MANY A WINDING TURN

A COLLECTION OF
REMEMBRANCES AND REVELATIONS

ALLEN COOK

CLAY BRIDGES
PRESS

Many a Winding Turn
A Collection of Remembrances and Revelations

Published by Clay Bridges Press in Houston, TX
www.ClayBridgesPress.com

ISBN: 978-1-68488-167-3
eISBN: 978-1-68488-168-0

Special Sales: Most Clay Bridges titles are available in special quantity discounts. Custom imprinting or excerpting can also be done to fit special needs. Contact Clay Bridges at Info@ClayBridgesPress.com

To my supporters and encouragers, with particular acknowledgments for my sister Evelyn Middleton of South Carolina; long-time encourager and confidante Susan Davis of Vermont; almost-best-friend Jeff Martin of Georgia; and my wife, Amy, favorite daughter of the Broad Run (West Virginia) community

Stories, of course, are common as dirt. Everyone has one, if not an infinity of them, and they surround us at all times whether we acknowledge them or not. Stories are the wells we dip into to be reminded of who we are.

—Jean Hanff Korelitz, *The Plot*

Your life will have 25,000 days in it. Make sure you remember some of them.

—Matt Haig, *The Humans*

TABLE OF CONTENTS

PREFACE

The stories in this book have been jotted down over the past twenty-five years and appear in chronological order, not by when they were written but by the days and years the memorable events occurred. An unintended consequence is that viewpoints and verb tenses occasionally (and haphazardly) flip to and fro from one story to the next. In addition, my writing style tends to fluctuate, along with my state of mind or subject matter. Please bear with me.

The described events, places, and people represent sixty years' worth of pain-filled lessons, startling epiphanies, curious encounters, calculated ponderings, evolving worldviews, vacillating priorities, chronic susceptibilities, and oft-compromised aspirations that have guided me along my breathtakingly nonlinear journey—or, more accurately, series of journeys.

Life is a journey, a road of subtle curves, sweeping vistas, daunting detours, and enticing side streets.

During my journey, I have from time to time brazenly upshifted into fourth gear with a sense of direction and a general idea of where I would like to end up, but the journey has always found ways to shift beneath me. It draws me in and compels me to reconsider my course and wonder whether the destination I imagined was meant for me. I have reached crossroads or forks that have demanded decisions—some large and looming, others quiet and almost imperceptible, their significance only clear in hindsight. But each choice, no matter how small, has left its mark, subtly altering the landscape ahead.

The irony is inescapable. I have spent the better part of twenty-five years creating and updating maps, meticulously charting pieces of the world line by line, polygon by polygon—only to be reminded that life itself has a way of wandering off the edges of the page entirely.

With welcomed benevolence, my journey surprises me with glimpses of breathtaking natural beauty, opportunities to forge connections with strangers, or afternoons of free-wheeled silliness with giggling grandchildren. These are the times when the journey feels like something more than a passage from one place to another—a conversation between me and the world, an unfolding and unveiling of my story (my mystery?).

My stories, directly or indirectly, involve scores of individuals, including more than a few strangers. Those folks, named or unnamed, represent a mere cross-section of my life's innumerable, effectual relationships. Companions have walked with me, some for only a mile or two, others for the long haul. Some have departed quietly, others abruptly, their absence noted but accepted. Others have left indelible impressions, their presence shaping not only my journey but my understanding of the road itself.

In most cases, the names of the folks who have found their way into my stories have been changed. In a few instances, time and place have been altered to ensure anonymity. These folks never asked to be portrayed in my disjointed, recorded ramblings.

As the sun on my gravel road begins to dip lower, casting the world around me in gradually fading light, I accept and even appreciate that the road will always have its bends and shadows, surprises and challenges. But within the twists and turns, there remains the providence of illustrious and unforeseen people, places, and events that continue to make the journey enjoyable, revealing, challenging, and inspiring—fortuitous rewards that beckon me onward with revelations and transformations waiting in the offing.

> *There's more than one answer to these questions, pointing me in a crooked line.*
>
> —Emily Saliers, fellow preacher's kid (PK)

FOR OPENERS . . .

A SNIPPET FROM MY GRANDMOTHER'S ORAL HISTORY

Near Chatom, Alabama, in the years before Prohibition lived an "Otis Campbell Prototype"—a fixture in and of the town's landscape, a man of indeterminate years, a study in denim, known to the locals as "Cully."

Cully was a bachelor farmer who spent his days working just beyond the outskirts of town. For many years, Saturday nights would find him at the town's lone watering hole. With this unwavering ritual, Cully earned a singular reputation for imbibing to excess. He was neither a mean drunk nor a violent drunk but would invariably find himself incapacitated in the early (and not so early) Sunday hours. Being aware of this propensity, Cully would plan accordingly. His early Saturday evening routine involved pushing his weather-beaten wheelbarrow into town and leaving it directly in front of the aforementioned drinking establishment.

With any luck, the comatose Cully would awaken to discover that some considerate soul had wheeled him home to his own front stoop. On less fortunate mornings, he would painstakingly greet the new day from his "parking spot" in town.

As the years passed, Cully's health, quite predictably, took a series of turns for the worse. Concurrently, his chronic cash-flow issues were encumbered by beer flow. Displaying admirable fortitude and unsuspected resolve, Cully surprised everyone, ceased his Saturday night forays, and resolutely climbed on the wagon.

A couple of years into Cully's sobered state, his wheelbarrow was discovered on a Saturday night near the doors of the town's bar. Word of the sighting spread quickly throughout the town and did not escape the notice of Chathom's self-appointed matriarch, moral compass, societal standard-bearer, and unrivaled dispenser of gossip: Miz Margaret.

Miz Margaret began by dialing the town's elected officials, clergy, and cotillion-veteran debutantes. As Garrison Keillor would later opine, "In a town this size, folks don't get their news from a newspaper. The newspaper is largely ceremonial."

Cully's measured response did not involve fighting fire with fire (or firewater). Nor did he opt for public confrontation. A summoning of witnesses? No. Cully had another quite inspired agenda. The following Saturday evening, he wheeled his barrow toward the town's center but stopped one and a half blocks short, leaving his single-wheeled conveyance in the neatly manicured front yard of Miz Margaret . . . for the night.

> *Don't judge a man by where he is, because you don't know how far he has come.*
>
> —C.S. Lewis

PART 1:

THE FORMATIVE YEARS (WESTERN NORTH CAROLINA)

THE CITY

My big sister Evelyn and I grew up in a series of small North Carolina towns: Tryon, Jamestown, Rutherfordton, Eden, and Mount Airy. While we enjoyed and certainly made the most of small-town life, we relished visits to our grandparents' home near the brightly lit city of Charlotte. The most prominent and enduring of a panoply of fond memories are three particular outings—one frequent, one seasonal, and one singular.

Frequent: Without regard to season or weather, and certainly without fail, each trip to our grandparents' house would feature at least one visit to the spectacle that was the automated car wash. Invariably, the washing process transfixed our senses. Squeals of delight would fill the car as our heads involuntarily pivoted in futile attempts to catch every movement within the 360-degree panorama of brushes, hoses, nozzles, and torrential showers. How clearly I remember our climbing from back seat to front and then back again in a frenzied effort to take in the sights, sounds, and smells. We were enveloped in sensory extravagance.

Seasonal: In mid-December, our mom and grandparents would bundle us into our pajamas early in the evening. Before venturing out, we would grab our winter coats and slide them on over our pajamas. Decades later, I recall being enamored by a feeling of daring secrecy. To the inattentive passersby, I would appear to be wearing my daytime attire . . . Ha!

Our grandfather would drive us through the night to the heart of the quiet city: Tryon Street at Trade Street. We would take in the season's magnificence creatively displayed in the Belk and Ivey's department store windows. Brilliant lights and colors lent their jolly aura to the entire block, if not the entire world, with Mr. and Mrs. Claus, a veritable herd of reindeer, radiant Christmas trees, legions of elves, and gift-wrapped boxes. My sister and I would peer at the store windows, suspended in amazement.

Singular: The event was a much-anticipated trip to the cavernous Charlotte Coliseum on Independence Boulevard, surely the largest structure I would ever encounter. Our grandparents were spoiling us once more by taking us to the circus. I remember leaving my grandfather's car in the boundless parking lot (how would we ever find his car again?) and feeling a rush of adrenaline as my grandmother grabbed our tiny hands in an act not only of safety but of a shared, unbridled exuberance. As she guided us to the imposing monstrosity, she broke into song: "I Want to Hold Your Hand." How providential to be escorted to the circus by our irrepressible grandmother as she cheerily warbled the Beatles' latest hit!

In retrospect, never have I felt more on top of the world.

> *The soul should always stand ajar, ready to welcome the ecstatic experience.*
>
> —Emily Dickenson

HIDDEN SHAME

Early one fall morning in 1966, my five-year-old self was moving about the house, preparing for the day's hectic schedule of duties and responsibilities. In the midst of my preparation for the demanding day at hand, the upstairs maid (referred to hereafter as "Mama") entered my bedroom and announced that due to bad planning, there were no clean undergarments for my use that day. The crux of the matter soon became obvious: Mama's Plan B was at loggerheads with my own Plan B. While I stridently lobbied for the eco-friendly option of "reuse," Mama remained steadfast in her position that such an option ran contrary to the letter and intent of several local (as well as state) laws. With time and scheduling constraints weighing on the decision-making process, Mama introduced an arrestingly implausible Plan B, a plan laden with far-reaching implications. Determinedly and solemnly, Mama announced that she would go to my older sister's room and bring back a pair of clean undergarments from her dresser drawer.

After the smelling salts had taken effect, I propped myself up on my bony elbows and informed Misguided Mama that such a plan was not a viable Plan B, C, D, or E by any stretch of decorum or ethics. Presented with a vastly insufficient period of time, I was unable to prepare a suitable defense. Small-town North Carolina . . . 1966 . . . googling "lingerie legal assistance" was hardly an option.

Emphatic, angst-ridden requests for phone calls to social services or local authorities were denied as I was man- (okay, woman-) handled and heaved headlong into the back seat of my mother's waiting Rambler station wagon. I pondered my grim and cruel fate as my driver (again, answering to "Mama") made her way to the place where my ridicule would be complete.

By the time we arrived at my kindergarten, I had convinced myself that the ruffles of the frilly white panties would manifest themselves through my cotton pants with a telltale luminescence—a glow that would make my wardrobe atrocity known to every man, woman, and child as I made my way down the echoing hallway to my classroom. Dead boy walking. Instinctively, I knew that even if my pants did not fall down during recess, my terrible secret would be discovered as I took a fraction of a second too long to "arrange things" at the urinal in the boys' bathroom. I would be forced to wear a scarlet letter ("P" for panties) to kindergarten for the foreseeable future.

Surely James, my bestest friend in the world, would realize something was amiss. Our (collective) four parents had been informing people in our little town that James and I were "joined at the hip." I feared that my friend would declare his own hips to be off limits when his young and impressionable ears heard the sordid news regarding my own hips and their adornment. Would Mrs. Greenwood, our kindly and devoted teacher, make notes in my permanent record? Would my always-scheming big sister broadcast the sordid tale at Millis Road Elementary School, thereby ruining any chance I might have to continue my education beyond the world of crayons, naps, finger painting, and graham crackers? For the duration of the morning, I contemplated cataclysmic scenarios and consequences along these lines.

After decades (many spent in therapy) of silence on the matter, I am now telling my story. You may wonder why I am doing so. It is a selfless act. The damage to my own psyche has been done. I write today to ask (nay, beg) young moms and dads to pause and consider the consequences of their decisions.

An early lesson for my life: the fear of being found out is a dance, a waltz of vulnerability and angst that all come to know in due time.

Trauma comes back as a reaction, not a memory.

—Bessel van der Kolk

WINN-DIXIE DAYS

My sainted mother loved the location of the Rutherfordton, North Carolina, parsonage, due in no small part to the cross-street neighbor, the Winn-Dixie. For a ten-year-old and a twelve-year-old in the house, this readily-accessible storehouse equated to a 6,000-square-foot pantry. Throughout my first four years in residence, I could count on at least one trip to the store each day. Few and far between were trips that did not include the purchase of a half-gallon carton of Sealtest milk (at 66 cents). Full gallons were available at $1.25, but Mama was willing to forgo the scant savings in the name of freshness. Sure, there was an outside chance that milk in that particular house might reach its expiration date, right up there with the chance that the next guy you see driving a Corvette will not be sporting a mustache.

She purchased Milky Way bars and in warmer weather refrigerated them and cut them into thirds—one for my mom, one for my sister, and one for me. Milky Way bars held scant appeal for my dad. His temptations were found elsewhere. He had committed to memory the precise latitude and longitude of every Russell Stover factory outlet store in the Carolinas.

Other regular Winn-Dixie purchases included Yelton's flour, Sunbeam bread, Peter Pan peanut butter, American cheese, bunches of bananas, and cubic yards of cereal. At that time in small-town North Carolina, available cheeses were American, cheddar, and (for those who could withstand the withering glances) Swiss. ("*Look* what is in her buggy, Gertie! I tell you, she's been straying from the path ever since she up and left the Naomi Circle.") Peanut butter and bananas were the cement and rebar of my food pyramid.

In the spring of that year, a marketing savant at United Brands headquarters in Cincinnati experienced an epiphany: ten-year-old American boys were, for all intents, keeping Chiquita solvent.

This same demographic was glued to TV sets every fall for NFL football. Thus ideas were hatched, executives were convinced, and for the next year, every bunch of Chiquita bananas featured the usual blue Chiquita sticker plus a round sticker with the name and logo of one of the NFL's twenty-six teams.

One warm and unprepossessing summer day when the first truckload of NFL-endorsed bananas hit the Rutherfordton Winn-Dixie, I happened to be picking up a few items in the causeway leading to "banana island." The result? The long love affair between boys and bananas had never seen—and would never again see—such unyielding devotion to banana-eating by a single 67-pound boy.

Each day, just after lunch, I would ask Mama if she needed anything from the store. With a weekly allowance of 25 cents, I was unequivocally incapable of supporting my own habit. I would have to rely on cunning and Mama's grocery budget.

"You sure you don't need anything? I see we are running low on spray starch." If no grocery items were needed, my fallback plan involved Coke bottles. One advantage to living on Main Street was that returnable Coke bottles were perpetually available. I crunched the numbers in my head and ascertained that one returned six-pack (worth a nickel) would pay for one banana. Thus, five six-packs would equal one bunch of bananas and . . . one prized sticker.

In actuality, my mother's private strategy enabled my own. Her creative mind had, I am convinced, been anything but idle. It is more than plausible that under layers of craft supplies, she had secreted an ambitious, meticulously crafted plan to convert her S&H Green Stamps cache into real estate—more specifically, a beach house.

Time flies like an arrow. Fruit flies like a banana.
—Groucho Marx

THE THINGS KIDS LEARN

In the fall of 1971, I was a fifth grader at Rutherfordton Elementary School, Mrs. Moore's class. Given the inclination, I could write about Mrs. Moore's teaching style for three days. To refer to it as "no-nonsense" would be to engage in impetuous understatement. According to quasi-documented rumors, she was wanted in four states (and two US territories) for child-o-cide. The cause of death for each victim simply read "index finger" or "malevolent glare." Had she been married to Andrew (Old Hickory) Jackson, her unyielding severity would have "toughened him up."

One autumn day, I left Mrs. Moore's class for a memorable, regrettable bathroom break, along with several other class members. Concurrently, a few kids from the other fifth-grade class were being released in consideration of the same bodily functions. What happened next was so jarringly unexpected that the thought of it unsettles me today.

North Carolina's public school integration was still in its early stages. The local Rutherfordton-Spindale Central High School was struggling mightily with the transition. Bomb threats and riots were not uncommon. It was a trying, turbulent time for teachers, parents, and students.

Our day-to-day existence had remained relatively quiet at the elementary school, and I had naively presumed that it would remain so . . . until I opened the door to the boys' room on that day of days. My sneakers had barely touched the bathroom tile when a fellow fifth grader grabbed my left hand and wrist. "Here's another White boy!" I was thrown against one wall with four other White boys. In my hypervigilant state, I surveyed the small room. I remember looking into the faces of the other boys lined up against two opposing walls. They showed uncertainty, fear, and confusion. Two boys, one White and one Black, were animated and agitated. It quickly became clear that they were the catalysts.

Standing with my bony shoulder blades against the cement block wall, I surveyed the room again. Not only had I no desire to fight but there was the added and supremely inconvenient fact that I had no idea how to fight. My only "fights" had been brief struggles with my older sister with lots of yelling, scratching, and slapping. Biting had been taken out of the equation years earlier. I had zero interest in fighting, especially with the boys who stood before me. They were my playground friends. How many softball, kickball, and basketball games had we played together with never so much as a shouting match? We ate lunches together. We rode bikes through the small town's quiet streets together. We spent countless afternoons at the community pool playing "sharks and minnows." We slept together in canvas pup tents during Boy Scout campouts. How had our network of friendships been rendered inconsequential?

My panicked thought process was interrupted by one of the instigators. "We are going to have our own race riot right here." Bespectacled boys were provided an opportunity to put their glasses away on the bathroom counter. A voice from one Black boy intervened. "Wait. This isn't fair. There are seven of us and only five of them." A second voice from the far side of the room responded. "Okay, hold on. I'll go fight with the White boys." Above all else was the desire to make this thing fair. A thought that dwelled with me the rest of the day and for years to come was this: the Event was about race, but to me, it had more to do with mimicking the big kids at the high school. We were trying to grow up fast and did not know how.

The bathroom walls reverberated with anxiety. Just as the two sides (now six apiece) were reluctantly in place, another boy raced in from the hallway. Word had somehow seeped out. "Guys! Knock it off! The principal is coming!" We scattered like proverbial rats. In fact, the principal was nowhere to be seen. I can't remember the name of the boy who burst in issuing his emphatic, false cry of alarm, but decades later, I remain thankful for his inventive interruption. Some days I wonder if the twelve of us would have ever come to blows. I fervently hope not.

I never told my parents or my teacher about the Event. It was years before I mentioned it to anyone. As far as the eleven other boys who participated in this staged bit of high drama, the Event was never mentioned again. I do remember not touching my lunch that day. I also remember having one of my fabricated "stomach aches" the following day as I convinced my mother that I was far too sick to attend school. As I remember, much of that melancholy day was spent sitting on my bed, staring out my window. In no small way, a large part of my carefree boyhood was . . . over.

> *The past is our definition. We may strive, with good reason, to escape it, or to escape what's bad in it, but we will escape it only by adding something better to it.*
>
> —Wendell Berry

SAMUEL

For whatever reason(s), fifth grade was an era of momentous events in my life. As the weeks played out, a slowly emerging realization was that I was, by no means, alone in this regard.

In the midst of a seemingly inconsequential winter's day, collective studies in my classroom were interrupted by a visitor. The halted-in-progress lesson was most likely a tale of yet another Spanish conquistador, regaled with disturbing fondness.

The visitor was Mrs. Baker, our school's special education teacher—a dedicated, patient, but clinically institutional woman with a high-pitched drawl. She gave our teacher a knowing look and then determinedly walked over to Samuel's desk. Samuel sat transfixed, hoping against hope that her footsteps would continue past his desk.

Mrs. Baker looked down at Samuel and announced to the whole world that Samuel would have the good pleasure of joining her in her classroom with all manner of activities awaiting. "You'll be my number one helper," she said. I had to look away as my ears registered the wailing entreaties from the unsuspecting ten-year-old boy, the panicked pleas, the stabs of despair to my own chest. Fifty years after this abject failure in procedure, I still see Samuel in my mind's eye—hands with white-knuckle grips on his desk, head down, tears streaming. After Samuel had absorbed this life-altering pronouncement, his denim jacket seemed two sizes too big. His face revealed a palpable sense of awareness that he would, with unconscionable abruptness, be removed from his comfortingly familiar surroundings.

Over the next couple of years, I would see Samuel in the lunch room or on the playground. We would exchange waves and smiles, but the Powers That Be had forever separated us with an invisible, unyielding divider. Even at that tender age, I knew on a primal level that what I had witnessed was inexcusable. Wrong. Horrific. Scarring. Misguided is much too nice a word.

Since that distant day, I have wondered: Did Samuel's parents know? Did my teacher know? Who made this decision? Why was Samuel's transition painfully lacking in consideration and compassion?

I am left with a lone resolution: to be aware of the Samuels who come into my life and make every effort to acknowledge and learn from them; and to have enough presence of mind to recognize that, at least on some days, I am Samuel.

> *You've developed the strength of a draft horse while holding onto the delicacy of a daffodil . . . you are the mother, advocate and protector of a child with a disability.*
>
> —Lori Borgman

LITTLE TOWN OF BETHLEHEM

Just short of my eleventh birthday, I traveled with my family to the Holy Land. It was an awe-inspiring, momentous experience for all, as we were fortunate enough to be able to visit the sites of pivotal biblical events. I had looked forward to the trip for a full year and had tried to envision myself standing at the Sea of Galilee, the Jordan River, Jacob's Well, the Mount of Olives, and more.

The place I was most eager to explore was the town of Bethlehem where the baby Jesus had been born. I had convinced myself that The Place would remain in use almost 2,000 years later as a stable—not just any stable, mind you, but a tranquil, full-scale, made-to-order Nativity Stable, complete with clean, becalmed animals ensconced in layer upon layer of fresh hay. Perhaps a few young shepherds would be peaceably assembled nearby.

What we found instead was a cement building. My family joined throngs of other pilgrims on the busy street outside as we awaited our turn to squeeze into a narrow, dimly lit stairway in order to take in the spectacle of . . . a basement. Not a sheep or donkey in sight.

I don't remember taking a single picture. The grey room represented the polar opposite of my expectations. I remember feeling deflated and confused. How could the site of such a miraculous event be reduced to a dank basement? Where was the stable—and the inn? Where was the newly fallen snow? Where was "love's pure light"?

Years later I reflected on that eventful day and my reaction. Slowly, I began to sympathize with the Israelites of Jesus's day. Their notions of the Messiah's arrival were so off base that most of them missed the foretold Savior—completely. In my childhood naiveté, I had traveled halfway around the world, expecting to find barnyard animals standing around a manger.

How many times in the following decades have I missed Jesus because He was not where I had been expecting to find Him?

> *Earth's crammed with heaven, and every common bush afire with God, but only he who sees takes off his shoes.*
>
> —Elizabeth Barrett Browning

JUST KEEP SWIMMING!

During the 1960s and 1970s, untold scores of American children scoffed at their parents' strident warnings and drowned while attempting to swim less than half an hour after eating. I never read about those drownings in the newspapers, but their cautionary tales made the rounds every time we kids even entertained notions of wading.

My mother was no more and no less vigilant than any other parent, camp counselor, lifeguard, responsible concerned citizen, or Scout leader. There was no gap in the ranks of their united, intractable front. Swimming less than a half hour after eating was risking death—death by debilitating stomach cramps. It was on the same risk level as handling venomous snakes, playing with loaded guns, failing to look both ways, climbing into a panel van with candy-laden strangers, or refusing to duck and cover.

Many a childhood afternoon the scenario played out in my head as I sat poolside. It was no stretch of my prodigious imagination to envision it all: An underparented (and predictably submersible) kid foolheartedly jumps in the deep end at the twenty-seven-minute mark and is immediately sucked into the murky depths with the force of a water spout. (I am alive today due to my mother's resolute watch for water spouts at Garden City Beach, South Carolina.)

Even into adulthood, whenever I hear news of drowning, my initial thoughts center on the half-hour rule. Natalie Wood: Quarter-pounder with cheese after twenty minutes? Dennis Wilson: Surf 'n turf at twelve minutes? Australian Prime Minister Harold Holt: Vegemite sandwich at the eighteen-minute mark?

None of us kids dared question this risk, although I did have a series of related questions for my mother considering the interpretation of the ironclad rule. "What if I only eat *half* of my hot dog? Could I get back in the water after fifteen minutes?" "I grabbed a handful of Joey's Fritos. That doesn't count, right?" Those questions were worth consideration from where I stood. My mother would crunch the pertinent metabolic calculations for each question, occasionally consulting with or receiving much-appreciated backup from a nearby parent.

At any rate, because of or in spite of the half-hour rule, my sister and I are alive and buoyant today.

> *Mothers don't sleep; they just worry with their eyes closed.*
>
> —Unknown Source

TO QUOTE BARNEY FIFE: "MY TRAUMATIC . . . TRAUMA"

My Great Uncle Ellis was my childhood Humor Tutor. Despite the fact that he struggled gamely with degenerative knees, he could detect, underscore, extrapolate, and utilize parts-per-billion traces of humor in any situation (oftentimes to the consternation of my exasperated Great Aunt Mary Frances).

Uncle Ellis and Aunt Mary Frances spent the bulk of their retirement years in a little two-bedroom cottage that Uncle Ellis built by hand, with help from my grandfather, in Garden City Beach, South Carolina. From his favorite rocking chair on the front porch, Uncle Ellis could listen to the waves, watch the passersby, and yell a "yes" or "no" to eager kids selling boxes of Krispy Kreme doughnuts door-to-door.

This front porch was the stage for The Trauma (at age twelve, many things are small-t traumatic).

I was sitting in "my" rocker, chatting with Uncle Ellis about friends back home, the weather, hush puppies, my grandparents, and a sprawling range of other subjects, when two tanned sixteen-year-old girls ambled past. They were dressed in typical 1970s beach clothing: halter tops and cut-off jeans with sewn-on patches. Both were stylishly shod in flip-flops. They did not escape notice of the twelve-year-old boy or the seventy-five-year-old man. Once the two chatty teens were directly in front of us, Uncle Ellis cut loose with a shrill, echoing wolf whistle. A nano-second later, his chin dropped to his chest in a practiced pose of mock sleep—his defining dramatic role: somnambulant septuagenarian.

There I sat, helplessly dumbstruck, eyes wide, mouth ajar. More than anything, I wanted to crawl under the cottage for the remainder of the 1970s. By the time I recovered and pointed a trembling index finger toward the guilty party, the girls had already turned, assessed, smiled, and moved on down South Waccamaw Drive.

Uncle Ellis never commented on the girls or my terror-stricken reaction. He merely offered a self-satisfied grin, winked, and then commented that we might get a little rain before supper.

> *A bolt from the blue. I have sometimes read of an unexpected event described in this way, and now I know exactly what is meant by the phrase. A blue sky, a sunny, mild day. . . . And then lightning strikes from out of that innocent blue sky and all that remains is the smoking ruins of one's every hope and every dream.*
>
> —Patrice Kindl

STAND AND DELIVER

Near the end of my four-year stay in Rutherfordton ("Ruv-tun"), I was seated in the New Hope School cafeteria, quietly enjoying my PB&J sandwich when I noticed my friend Johnny stand abruptly at a neighboring table. The topic of conversation remains a mystery to everyone not seated at Johnny's table, but a line had been crossed.

When the normally calm and circumspect friend rose from his chair, nearly everyone in the cafeteria turned to hear his pronouncement: "I can't listen to this. You are talking 'bout folks who ain't here to defend themselves. Hurtful words. It ain't right. I can't be a part of this."

After pushing his chair under the table, he turned on his heel and walked outside where he sat on a concrete wall until the lunch hour came to an end, gazing at the ballfield and the piney woods beyond. Others would ask Johnny about the topic of conversation and his vehement reaction. On each of those occasions, Johnny would respond with a shake of the head and sealed lips.

This singular act of defiant resolve has stayed with me over the decades. Johnny's words have served as a reminder to me whenever I find myself party to discussions of a similar nature. From time to time, I have left the metaphorical table, but never with Johnny's heartfelt firmness of conviction.

> *Be sure you put your feet in the right place, then stand firm.*
>
> —Abraham Lincoln

FIRST CONTACT

Moving every fourth year would be tough on any kid. Junior high years are terrifying for everyone.

For the trifecta, let's relocate a junior high kid who happens to be an introvert.

For Methodist pastors and their families, arduous, disorienting moves took place in mid-June. The opportunity to meet fellow students in new schools would not occur until late August. Hence, every fourth year of my childhood delivered a Summer of Loneliness.

For the month of June 1973, my parents, my sister, and I were spending our waking hours unpacking boxes, attempting to make yet another parsonage our home at 511 Patrick Street. Midway through my 216th box, the phone in the hallway rang. Against all odds, the phone call was for me. Wait, what? We had only been in town for a week. Who on earth would be asking for me? Intrigued, curious, and doubtlessly welcoming any diversion, I clambered to the phone.

On the other end of the line was Jim, a fellow twelve-year-old I had met briefly at church that Sunday. Wasting no time, Jim asked if I wanted to head over to the YMCA to shoot some baskets. The invite was monumental. Initially, it meant deliverance from the corrugated labor camp that had become my life. Metaphorically, it was my door to an infinitely wider world.

Jim seemingly knew every man, woman, and child at the Y, as well as every square inch (sparing the girls' locker room) of the facility. Thanks to Jim's timely invite, I would get to know dozens of kids who would become my classmates that fall.

The morning after The Phone Call, my mother was by my side at the Y's front desk, asking for a membership form. To the inattentive layperson, it might even have appeared that my mother had leaped at the chance to remove her youngest, most endearing offspring from under foot.

That summer was a blur of basketball, swimming, tennis, ping pong, and a made-up gym game that was part basketball, part football, and part volleyball. As I recall, YMCA stalwart Jerry was the game's primary architect. As for our pool activities, swimming was admittedly not the primary focus. Jumping, splashing, and cooling off were. (Lifeguard Phyllis can bear witness.)

Summer days at the YMCA led to church-league softball, neighborhood bike rides, and basketball tournaments in the Myotts' driveway—with the same core participants. It is not possible for me to overstate the lifelong impact that group of like-minded, even-keeled, good-humored, energetic friends had on me. They were there for me when I was supremely daunted, impressionable, and vulnerable.

I am a daily witness to countless little dramas of growth, judgment, healing, friendship, sacrifice, reconciliation, miracles, and rebirth—in short, the central themes of the Gospel.

—Garrison Keillor

RAINY NIGHT IN SHEA STADIUM, UNDAMPENED SPIRITS

In June 1977, I was on full sensory overload. Three high school friends and I were at Shea Stadium, excitedly chatting as the Mets prepared to take on the visiting Phillies. Thanks to one friend's cousin, Ron Hodges (at that time the backup catcher for the Mets), we were perched in family box seats behind home plate. It felt as if we had stepped into the heart of baseball itself.

Decades later I am amazed by the number and clarity of memories from that night. Craig Swan, the closest thing the post–Tom Seaver Mets had to an ace, was pitching. His wife and three-year-old daughter occupied the seats in front of us. The precocious tot would periodically stand in her seat and yell, "Strike 'em out, Daddy!" Priceless. An intoxicating atmosphere swirled around me. "Methodist PK takes symbolic step for total immersion. Film at 11:00."

I remember forgoing the ballpark hot dogs. I was much too excited to eat.

I remember watching the arching flight of a ball hit by Greg Luzinski into the left-field bleachers and wondering if I would ever again see a baseball hit that hard.

I remember being escorted through two security gates during the rain delay. As the four of us approached the Mets' locker room door, we were cautiously assessed by (cleatless) pitcher Nino Espinosa. If I had known how close Mets coach Willie Mays was to me at that moment in time, I would have collapsed on the rain- and beer-soaked cement. Of that, I am sure.

I remember being amazed by the defensive prowess of Gary Maddox as he, for all intents, covered center field and left field.

I remember Bruce Boisclair in right field making long strides to grab a sinking line drive, each footfall splashing water up over his blue stirrups.

I remember a man in his sixties seated across the aisle from us. As the delayed game extended into the sodden New York night, a half-dozen large beers transported the man to a Giants game at the long-since-demolished Polo Grounds. At one point, the inebriated fan called for Dusty Rhodes to pinch hit.

After the rain-delayed game, the four of us piled into a subway car and headed back to the bright lights of Times Square. It was well past midnight, and we clung to the metal poles of the rattling train, determined to look like we belonged. To this day, I'm convinced that no group of sixteen-year-olds ever tried harder to pull off an air of calm, cool indifference. We stood there with all the nonchalance we could muster while our wide eyes darted from one end of the car to the other. We were four boys from a sleepy mill town introduced to The City That Never Sleeps.

Once a year or so I pull out The Baseball—signatures of all the Mets. Some were illegible thirty-five years ago, and others have faded or disappeared over time. I don't need this tangible object for verification that the events happened or to evoke the memories from that night any more than I need the tag on Sallie's collar to tell me who she is.

> *People ask me what I do in winter when there's no baseball. I'll tell you what I do. I stare out the window and wait for spring.*
>
> —Rogers Hornsby

TEEN ROUTINES

During my early teen years, an outing with my Eden friends often involved a pressed-into-service parent with a station wagon and a trip to one of Greensboro's shopping malls—either Four Seasons or Carolina Circle. The Designated Parent (who had earlier drawn a short straw) would drop us off at one entrance and give instructions for a pickup time.

Our stops were predictable: the Record Bar, Spencer's Gifts, sporting goods stores, and the food court. Mostly, we weren't shopping so much as practicing how to exist in public. We would observe teen girls in their loose clusters, chattering like exotic birds, and though we admired dozens from afar, we spoke to a grand total of zero. It was as if we were watching a documentary about a species whose mating calls we had not yet learned.

Although we spent some of our time assessing the clothing on display, we were merely window shopping. In those bygone years, the actual purchasing of clothing involved factory stores at the local textile mills.

About the time these same friends and I acquired our drivers' licenses, I was abruptly relocated to Mount Airy. With state-issued licenses to explore, my newfound friends and I established a new (to us) routine: driving down US-52 to Winston-Salem to take in a litany of acclaimed (and not-so-acclaimed) moving pictures.

Sure, Mount Airy had its own movie theater: the Mayberry Cinema. The problem was that this establishment was limited to a single screen. Once we had taken in the local offerings, we would have to wait an interminable amount of time for a new arrival. Particularly vexing was *Coal Miner's Daughter* starring Sissy Spacek and Tommy Lee Jones. The movie arrived one spring day and played nightly on the cinema's screen for, well, heck, it may still be playing. Sissy may still be belting her little heart out, waiting for someone to tell her she's free to go home.

In Winston-Salem, we would share popcorn, make witty asides during the movie (at least witty to us) and then, like pilgrims on a holy march, head directly to Krispy Kreme on South Stratford Road. If the neon HOT NOW sign happened to be aglow, we'd enter a realm of glazed ecstasy—one box for the front seat, one for the back.

By the time we reached the Pilot Mountain exit, the feeding frenzy would be over, doughnuts having been replaced by regret. The final 10 miles of the journey would consist of box-licking. To my knowledge, the only variance in this northbound, calorie-saturated return to port involved two screeching left turns and an unscripted hideout behind a barn. Suffice it to say that Surry County's only Peugeot was seeking some quiet time away from an alert state trooper.

I often pause to consider the science behind the Highway Patrol's Doughnut Detector.

> *You never have the sort of friends you have when you're fifteen ever again. Even if you keep them for the rest of your life, it's never the same as it was then.*
>
> —Fredrik Backman

LONG OVERDUE THANK YOU . . . TO MOUNT AIRY

A note of appreciation that is as insufficient as it is tardy: In the late 1970s, I was, for two years, a year-round resident of Mount Airy, North Carolina. I grudgingly moved from Eden to Mount Airy with my family after my sophomore year of high school. The uprooting that accompanies and underscores the moving process never fails to confound, disorient, and exacerbate, especially when a new school is involved. I would have to adjust to new surroundings—once again. Such is the lot in life when you are a Methodist preacher's kid.

Two months after arriving in town, my family was involved in a head-on collision on a lonely stretch of Highway 601 south of town. Three people, including my mother and a dear family friend, would not survive. My father's physical recovery would take more than a year. My sister and I, also hospitalized, were left to wonder where (in our unfamiliar surroundings) we would go when the time came for our hospital discharge.

Five different families in Mount Airy got word to us that we would have living options. Relative strangers opened their homes to us without fuss, condition, or timetable. We were—and still are—overcome with gratitude. Other folks soon volunteered to drive us to physical therapy, church, and Winston-Salem's Baptist Hospital to visit our father. Our needs were lovingly and selflessly met at every turn.

Growing up, I always dreaded the first day in a new school. Throughout my physical and emotional recovery from the car accident, I viewed my upcoming introduction to life at Mount Airy High School with unsettling dread and foreboding. Several times a day, I envisioned walking to my first class alone with my back in a brace, my left arm in a cast, stitches on my face, and broken blood vessels in my eyes. No one needed to inform me that I was a sight to behold, a beleaguered study in plaster. My older sister would soon be headed off to college, so she would not "have my back" this time.

Thankfully, due to the effective and efficient small-town networking of our new friends and neighbors, I did not have to explain my condition or appearance to anyone. My story had preceded me. Each and every day, classmates, teachers, and staff members went out of their way to make me feel welcome and included in my new school.

Scholastically, allowances flowed liberally since I had missed the first two months of classes. Looking back on this time in my life, it remains abundantly clear that an appreciable number of other allowances were made. On more than one occasion, I took full advantage of my situation and, I confess, used my pity-inducing circumstances to my advantage. The good graces of Mount Airy's residents continued unabated.

Over the years, college and a series of jobs have led me away from the townspeople who freely shared their heartfelt concern and boundless encouragement. Although I only lived in Mount Airy briefly, I never hesitated to identify The Granite City as my hometown. I am proud and simultaneously humbled to be identified with the town whenever an opportunity presents itself. Blessings on the good people of Mount Airy.

These days, I only make it back to Mount Airy every couple of years or so. However, I visit much more regularly in my thoughts.

> *It's never far from wherever you are and when you go it never leaves you. You sit alone and thoughts of home come and stand around your chair.*
>
> —Garrison Keillor

PART 2:
THE 1980S (DURHAM, NORTH CAROLINA, AND METRO ATLANTA)

BEACH BENEVOLENCE

Charles, a close friend from high school, and I took advantage of a three-day weekend and headed to Myrtle Beach. Charles was always up for a beach trip, as was I for that matter.

Upon arrival, we checked into our hotel and scurried across the street to a convenience store for junk food and other necessities. After dodging the traffic on North Ocean Boulevard, Charles and I turned our gazes upon a woman sitting on the concrete stoop just beyond the reach of the store's air conditioning. Neither of us mentioned her. She had the bearing of a thirty-year-old who had led a tormented life. Her head leaned against a humming ice machine as her vacant eyes stared blankly in the general direction of the gas pumps. Her brown hair was matted, and her sparse clothing was soiled and tattered. A threadbare tank top left little to the imagination; the cut-off jean shorts showed more patches than denim.

I glanced down at her. My best thoughts were filled with pity. My worst thoughts were full of smug deprecation. I was destined to play the Levite in this little parable.

Charles walked over to the woman and offered a cheery "hello." She warily nodded. He chatted with her momentarily and learned that her name was Angie. Their conversation was low and subdued, but I was able to get the gist of it. Charles was relating that she looked as though she could use some rest and a good meal or two. Angie offered little in the way of response.

When Charles offered her a room in the hotel for the long weekend, she shook her head adamantly, fixing him with a piercing look. Her eyes replied, "Been there, done that." It took a good five minutes of solemnity for Charles to convince her that she would have her own room, would hold the only key, and could order room service. No ulterior motives. No plans for a beach-side dalliance.

We saw Angie in the hotel hallway a couple of times during our stay. On Monday morning, we said goodbye and exchanged well wishes. Despite my self-righteous misgivings, I was keenly aware that Charles' condition-free generosity had left its mark on Angie. It certainly affected me.

> *The purpose of human life is to serve, and to show compassion and the will to help others.*
>
> —Albert Schweitzer

NOVEMBER EPIPHANY

One unprepossessing night in November 1980, I was walking from the Engineering Library to catch the campus bus when I paused to focus my attention on something, or rather someone. I was crossing Science Drive when it became apparent that I was being followed. The wooded path leading to the campus's center was exceedingly well-lit. In point of fact, it was a veritable tunnel of light. The unintended consequence of this abundance of wattage was that anyone lurking in the woods could make out every detail of anyone plodding along the path. In contrast, anyone on the path would remain clueless as to who or what might be perched in the surrounding darkness.

A few moments earlier I had observed a young woman in the library as she packed up her books and grabbed her coat. However, she had not budged from her seat. With deductive logic that would have impressed Hercule Poirot, I surmised that she was waiting for someone. As the scene unfolded, I discovered that the "someone" was me.

As I made my way along the path, I could hear her light footsteps 30 feet or so behind me. My first thought was to turn and face her, to ask if she would like for me to walk with her. Realizing that such an action could easily have the opposite of its intended effect, I continued on my way. She followed me all the way to the bus stop where she ventured off in the wake of a boisterous gaggle of students headed to the dorms beyond.

After her departure, I sat on the bench to await the East Campus bus. Scanning my surroundings, I noticed a lighted window in the distance. A glow was coming from a third-floor classroom within the gargantuan Perkins Library—a beacon from a welcoming space. The room on the opposite side of the window was my favorite study hideaway for three primary reasons: It was entirely free from distractions, it was usually unoccupied, and its aforementioned window afforded a view of a magnolia (my favorite tree). On nights when this space beckoned me, I would climb the back stairs of the library to the third floor and then follow a silent maze of hallways to my sanctuary's weighty oak door.

Until the scales fell from my eyes that night, I had never given a moment's consideration of whether the Engineering Library or my secluded sanctuary would be a safe place to study (day or night).

I'm hoping for similar epiphanies this day, especially for members of the Old Guard.

> *It's the everyday things women go through that breed this fear of being alone at night.*
>
> —Claudia, age 19

MISS LULU

The main reason I preferred life on Duke's East Campus was the relative quiet. West Campus was, in comparison, a three-ringed circus. East Campus was also closer to downtown Durham, Parker's Diner, Swenson's ice cream shop, and the Durham Athletic Park ("The DAP").

From my dorm, I could embark on a pleasant stroll through hushed, tree-lined neighborhoods, past Durham High School, over the railroad tracks, then up a well-worn footpath to The DAP, the venerable home of the Durham Bulls. On a couple of occasions, friends and I took advantage of off-nights and snuck onto the infield under cover of gathering darkness. There we would take turns standing at home plate, bat in hand, merrily swatting old golf balls over the outfield fence, over the tobacco warehouses, deep into the night—pretending to be storied Kings of the Diamond.

When the Bulls were in town, of course, we would take our seats and cheer on each season's unique blend of young, rough-hewn, "Single-A" talent. Several hitters and pitchers from this era made it to "The Show"—Albert Hall, Brett Butler, Brad Komminsk, Paul Zuvella, and Milt Thompson. (Brian Snitker came to bat only

780 times in his brief minor league career but now has his World Series ring as a manager.) For others, a season in Durham would prove to be the glimmering apex of their professional careers.

In September of my junior year, a friend and I were heading out to catch one of the last few games in the Bulls' 1981 season. We were ambling down Minerva Avenue when we were approached by an elderly woman in her "house coat." "Are you boys on your way to the ball game? Could I interrupt you for a moment?" Mrs. Wilkerson introduced herself and sheepishly explained that she had locked herself out of her house. "And I have a casserole in the oven," she added. "I have neighbors here, but I'm afraid they are even older and wobblier than I am."

Pete and I quickly offered our assistance. Mrs. Wilkerson breathed a sigh of relief and then stopped short. "Oh dear, I don't even have any ID or papers with me to prove that this is my house." Pete replied that if Mrs. Wilkerson ended up in jail that night, we would gladly accompany her.

Pete and I walked around to the shade of a sweetgum in Mrs. Wilkerson's backyard where we paused, hands on our chins. In an impressively short span of time, Pete focused his attention on the sliding glass doors that led to the back porch. He turned to deliver a knowing glance and then started for the porch. Pushing upwards with ten strong fingers, Pete gently raised the left sliding door a fraction of an inch and then motioned for me to help slide it to the right. We entered the porch from the doorway and were rewarded with an unlatched window.

We met Mrs. Wilkerson in her front yard. Pete addressed her: "The good news? It was a piece of cake getting into your house. The bad news? It is a piece of cake to get into your house."

She thanked us profusely and then sent us on our way, but not before giving us literal pieces of cake (poundcake), thoughtfully wrapped in paper napkins. In return, we gave her our phone numbers. "If you need a helping hand—a light bulb changed, a hinge oiled, whatever."

The following day, Pete and I received telephoned invitations for Saturday lunch. Swayed by the appeal of a home-cooked meal, we gladly accepted the invites.

When Saturday rolled around, we were invited in (the front door) to pot roast, hot cornbread, sweet tea, and some history. Mrs. Wilkerson explained that her late husband had sold life insurance for North Carolina Mutual and that she had worked in the secretarial pool at the American Tobacco Company. She was in the midst of her eighty-first year as a resident of Durham. "When I was a little girl in pigtails," she told us, "the Bulls played their home games on your East Campus." Pete and I were unaware of that fact. "Oh, yes. Hanes Field. Duke used to play all of their home football and baseball games there as well."

She recalled the fateful night in 1939 when the Durham Athletic Park structures all burned to the ground. "Awful night," she said. "Amazing to think that no lives were lost. My Stan and I walked over to the high school parking lot to watch the firefighters. And just a couple of years later, of course, they played the Rose Bowl here in Durham. Stan's company managed to get a couple of tickets for us."

Near the end of the meal, Mrs. Wilkerson recalled her years as a student on the UNC campus. "My first name is Louise, but all my college friends called me 'Lulu,'" she added wistfully. She paused to consider us. "Enough of this Mrs. Wilkerson business. Would you humor an old woman and call me Miss Lulu?" I still smile when I pause to remember her high-pitched, unrestrained laugh.

We stopped by, individually or in tandem, to visit Miss Lulu when time permitted. In return, she would phone us periodically. As far as immediate family, Miss Lulu had two children who lived on the West Coast and called her regularly. I can't begin to explain how moved I was on one of our afternoon visits when I took notice of the telephone contact list taped to Miss Lulu's kitchen wall—between the rotary-dial phone and the Autumn Gold range. The handwritten list featured the names of her children, a couple of neighbors, . . . along with Pete's and mine.

A year later, Miss Lulu sold her house and moved to California to be near her children. Dementia had begun to intrude on her day-to-day activities. Pete and I offered mock offense that she would choose blood relatives over us.

Over the decades, I have made infrequent trips back to Durham. When an occasion presents itself to visit the Bull City, I often walk around the East Campus wall. If time permits, I drive by the historic ballpark. One constant remains—taking a moment to peek down Minerva Avenue and offer thanks for a fortuitous encounter, a benevolent soul, and a kind-hearted neighbor.

> *The view from farther up the road is not better or more beautiful. It's not even always more accurate or right. But it's a view we simply cannot have from where we are.*
>
> — Julie Rybarczyk

AN ISLAND

In the winter of 1982–1983, I was a senior in college. For my final year, I retreated to a quiet neighborhood a mile south of Duke's East Campus. A young family of four lived on the two main floors of the imposing 6,600-square-foot house. The third floor was my safe haven: a living room, bathroom, and bedroom accessed by an opulent, winding, wooden staircase. In short, it was a glorious perch for a reflective introvert.

One Saturday morning in December I awoke to a rare sight for Durham. An overnight storm had silently blanketed the city with 5 inches of snow. My landlords and their children were away for the weekend, so I was already relishing the morning's silent stillness even before I ventured a glance from the third-floor window.

After my morning bowl of Cheerios (shared with Ralphie, the black Labrador in residence), I placed needle to vinyl and listened to the Simon and Garfunkel album *The Sound of Silence*. I then returned to the living room window to take in the wintry landscape and ponder several things, including my arduously fruitless attempts to formulate a plan for post-graduation life. There were exciting but nonetheless unnerving possibilities.

On that pivotal morning, it seemed that the vast majority of my contemporaries were beneficiaries of meticulously crafted personal goals, lofty aspirations, and clear-cut pathways, complete with chapter and verse. Though I knew better, I nonetheless began a stroll down Comparison Avenue. Catching myself, I shook off my discouragement and accepted what would later become Count Alexander Rostov's conclusion: Imagining myself in different circumstances was the surest path to madness. My personal corollary? Comparing myself to my own contemporaries was the surest path to melancholy.

In the preceding months, my sister (in July) and my father (in November) had settled down with their respective new spouses. My life was fast approaching a crossroads with no job prospects, no career path, no girlfriend, no option of returning home, and faltering confidence. Words from the poet Stephen Dobyns came to me: "Between my present and future was a wall so big that not even sunlight crossed over."

More than anything, I wanted to take my newly inked diploma in hand and resolutely follow it to the horizon—not just any horizon but my very own horizon.

Paul Simon's lonesome voice soon flagged down my distressed train of thought. "I am a Rock." A December day. Alone. There I stood, taking in the new snow from my upstairs window. Haunting parallels from every verse. Was I a rock? An island?

Initially, I was swept away in a current of startled unease. After a contemplative pause, I caught myself and smiled. I was in good company. It was reassuring to know that by no means was I the first to grapple with uncertainty.

> *The best thinking begins and ends with the wisdom of being unsure.*
>
> —Maggie Jackson

NIGHT OF FORTUNES

One night in the mid-1980s I cautiously but resolutely ventured forth on a first date with a young woman from Lincolnton, North Carolina. We ended up at a Chinese restaurant in nearby Hickory (pronounced "Hik-ry"). Hickory and Chinese food—hard to imagine one without the other, right?

Anyway, "things" were going okay for a first date—for me (quite the qualifier). At any rate, it was going much better than an episode a couple of years earlier when I made the tragic and never-to-be-repeated mistake of ordering BBQ ribs on a first (and last) date. Ah, but that is another story, one involving handfuls of napkins. At any rate, not even within the most charitable stretches of my imagination could I have been considered a suave Man About Town.

Tangent. Sorry. Back to the Chinese restaurant. At the end of the meal, the waitress came over with our fortune cookies. I opened my cookie and partially stifled a laugh. Susan noticed and quickly asked about my humorous fortune. I read from my slip of paper: "Tonight is yours. Be bold." She responded with a burst of laughter and handed me the fortune from her cookie: "Remember what your mother told you."

To this day, I can't help but wonder if our waitress had astutely surmised by our self-conscious behavior that this was a first date and had mischievously leaped at the opportunity to have a bit of fun with us. Touché!

If you think there are no new frontiers, watch a boy ring the front doorbell on his first date.

—Richard Miller

WHO IS MY NEIGHBOR?

I hesitate to share this story because it is not mine to tell. After much deliberation, I decided to describe the following conversations as I remember them. My neighbor's story made an indelible impression on me, and it has been cycling between my conscious and subconscious for decades, clearly wanting out. (The name of my neighbor, as well as the name of his hometown, have been changed out of respect for my neighbor's privacy.)

For sixteen months (1984 into 1985), I lived in an apartment in Clarkston, Georgia, next door to a solitary man named Jerry. We remained strangers for the first few months, exchanging cursory greetings of nods and smiles. After returning home from dinner at a nearby restaurant one evening, I found Jerry sitting outside—the first such sighting for me. He asked if I would like a beer. In response, I held up my leftover iced tea and asked if my caffeine and I could join him. We chatted about the weather and other innocuous topics for half an hour before I excused myself.

The following weekend we bumped into each other while picking up our mail. As we walked, we contemplated the

Braves' prospects. Seemingly out of the blue, Jerry, rather embarrassingly, asked if I had ever heard strange noises coming from his apartment in the middle of the night. A bit taken aback, I stated that I had not. "Okay, good. Just checking," he said. After a moment of awkward silence, we headed for our adjacent front doors. I closed my front door as I wondered aloud about Jerry's question.

A couple of weeks passed before we again spoke at any length. As if on cue, Jerry explained the reason for his unusual question. "You see, I was in 'Nam. Some nights, I wake from some . . . disturbing dreams."

I remember thinking, "Disturbing. Now there is a euphemism."

Gradually, we got to know each other over the course of months—Jerry the recluse and Allen (me) the introvert. Jerry was a diesel mechanic by day and a movie theater projectionist by night. "I work two jobs because . . . um 'cause I don't do well with time on my hands." I tried my best not to be intrusive or to press for details. Jerry was understandably guarded.

One interest we happened to share was an unrestrained keenness for the fare at Matthew's Cafeteria (in the nearby community of Tucker). Jerry: "Reminds me of home." I readily agreed. Once a month or so we would make the short pilgrimage there. On a couple of occasions, I asked Jerry if he might be interested in (church-league) softball or basketball. "No thanks." Later, I asked Jerry if he would like to go to church with me. He declined politely but firmly. I explained that many Vietnam veterans attended. "That may well be," he said, "but God abandoned me years ago."

From there, Jerry went on to describe his childhood in Gary, Indiana, and how he had lost his mother to cancer when he was the tender age of ten. "Six years later, The Horse (heroin) took my dad," Jerry added. He had no siblings. "I quit school at age sixteen and worked as a short-order cook in a local diner. The owner of the place had known my dad, so he let me sleep in the storage room. It turned out I was good at killing rats." Jerry also mentioned a junior high school teacher who would stop in at the diner on weekends to grab a burger and check on Jerry. "That," (Jerry took a deep breath) "meant the world to me."

In 1968, soon after his eighteenth birthday, Jerry was drafted into the Army and found himself a world away from Indiana. In our conversations, Jerry made it clear that he would only share his Vietnam experiences with fellow combat veterans. I nodded my solemn understanding. One revealing peek into his distant world was a singular late-night admission: "Once you find yourself holding an M16, trying to shoot a guy who is trying to kill you, there's just no way to get back home again. There's no 'reset' button to hit."

As Jerry had anticipated, I had no response. Not in the tiniest way could I begin to relate to his tour of duty. Every now and then during moments when I wallow in self-indulgence, I pretend that I have some vague notion of what it would be like to be the father of a child. Putting myself in Jerry's boots? Not a chance. I can't get there from here.

If I opened my mouth, I knew I would come off as patronizing, ignorant, insensitive, or gratingly curious. Instead, my response was to share the story of losing my mother (and very nearly my dad) a few months after my sixteenth birthday—some common ground to share in that realm.

In the weeks that followed, Jerry talked a bit about a new (1980) diagnosable condition known as post-traumatic stress disorder. "I checked every damned box," he said. One spring evening after we had returned home from a late-night visit to the Waffle House, Jerry (with more than a little hesitation) invited me into his apartment. He showed me a sampling of his art therapy and explained how it was helping him cope. "My talent, or lack of it, is not the point." Jerry also showed me his journal. The second half of the book was blank. The first half had been torn out, page by page. "I write about . . . things, then wait a day, read what I wrote, then burn the pages."

Jerry moved to Florida in November 1985. "If I belong anywhere, maybe it's there."

In the winter of 1987-1988, Jerry stopped replying to my letters. I later learned that he had died from a cerebral hemorrhage. When I think back on time spent at my old apartment, I always picture Jerry moving silently from his F-150 to his front door, lunch pail in hand.

Hoping you have found a place to call home, friend. You deserve that as much as anyone I have ever known.

> *"The brave men and women, who serve their country and as a result, live constantly with the war inside them, exist in a world of chaos. But the turmoil they experience isn't who they are; the PTSD invades their minds and bodies."*
>
> —Robert Koger

DEEP IN THE HUNDRED-ACRE WOOD

In the summer of 1987, Nick and I were exploring the Canadian Rockies. We had rented a car and were driving north from Banff National Park to Jasper National Park when we happened upon a car that had come to a stop along the side of the road. "Bear!" we exclaimed simultaneously. Sure enough, as we slowed to investigate, we spotted a young, lone grizzly digging in the dirt a mere 200 feet from the road.

As we drew closer, we noticed that the parked car's rear doors were open. A brother and sister, roughly ages six and eight, had abandoned the relative safety of the car and were standing in the grass, yelling things at the preoccupied bear, all the while (get this) throwing rocks in its direction. The clueless parents remained in the car, carelessly consulting a park map. I could imagine the conversation. "I'm not sure, Bobby. Should we check out the visitor's center next or stop at this little bakery?" Doubtless, they had given their eminently replaceable offspring permission to "go play with Winnie-the-Pooh."

Nick (a pediatrician) and I pondered courses of action. I was hoping against hope that his extensive training would not be put to the test in the immediate future. Less than a minute later, we were overcome with relief at the sight of an approaching park ranger's Jeep. The ranger briskly ushered the provocative children back into the family car and then turned and unleashed a vehement diatribe (as vehement as a Canadian can get) at the clueless parents.

I may well have imagined it, but I could almost have sworn that I caught a brief, nonverbal, mutually appreciative exchange between bear and ranger.

> *Those who have packed far up into grizzly country know that the presence of even one grizzly on the land elevates the mountains, deepens the canyons, chills the winds, brightens the stars, darkens the forest, and quickens the pulse of all who enter it.*
>
> —John Murray

PART 3:
THE 1990S (GREATER BURLINGTON, VERMONT)

C'EST MON CŒUR QUI TE PARLE (IT'S MY HEART THAT SPEAKS TO YOU)

Over the winter of 1988–1989, I applied to several graduate schools in the eastern United States. Letters of acceptance arrived from the University of Tennessee, the University of South Carolina, and the University of Vermont. After visiting the three campuses, I chose Vermont—not just the school but the entire state. One of the deciding factors was the allure of an unexplored vantage point. I wanted to experience life beyond my "backyard." A second (and overwhelming) factor was the setting. Since I would be spending years studying nature, I would be hard-pressed to find a more beguiling and inspiring locale.

In June 1989, I loaded up Virgil (my first Volvo) and headed north. As way led on to way (apologies, Mr. Frost), the alluring Green Mountain State would be my home for the next nine years. Invaluable assistance in the geo-transitioning process was provided by my ABF (Almost Best Friend) Jeff who mailed boxes to me emblazoned with the words "Grits Across America."

Inexplicably, Vermont grocery stores were lacking in regard to this most essential of dietary (sacramental?) staples.

After the 1,150-mile move, Jeff's ABF duties were partially assumed by a new acquaintance: Gary. Gary proved to be a steadfast friend, a reliable classmate, and the school's unrivaled connoisseur of Ben & Jerry's offerings. During our time together, both in the woods and on the bouncing bench seat of a rumbling Chevrolet K-10, I learned quite a bit about wildlife behavior. Gary would say, "These coyote tracking collars? No skimping. We buy top-of-the-line batteries because you can never trap a coyote a second time. Zero chance for swapping out batteries." "Ospreys won't build a nest if the platform we are building isn't rock-solid. An osprey platform can sway a bit in the wind but has to support at least 300 pounds. The two of us will test this platform when we are finished."

In addition to being a fountain of knowledge, Gary was a kindred spirit. He, too, was a recovering PK; his dad had served a procession of small churches in upstate New York and northern Vermont. One breezy autumn day as we took a break from setting up a nesting box for wood ducks, Gary, choked with emotion, shared a story from his late father's life. My attempt at capturing the events will undoubtedly lack Gary's personal touches, but I will take up the torch.

Phil, Gary's dad, had served seven years at a church situated amongst the idiosyncratic populace of Vermont's fabled Northeast Kingdom. In short order, Phil met the "movers and shakers" of the church, spearheaded by Isabelle, a young EMT who devoted an inordinate amount of her time helping out with various activities in and around the church—baking, befriending, gardening, encouraging, delivering, mending—basically whatever needed doing.

Days after meeting Phil, Isabelle popped by his office on the off chance that he might share an "occupational proclivity" toward brownie consumption. He would. He decidedly would.

A confectionary foundation for a budding friendship had been laid. Isabelle would become a frequent guest of Phil (and his wife, Denise), as well as a willing sounding board and dispenser of local knowledge.

As pastors are wont to do, Phil soon inquired about Isabelle's family. An only child, Isabelle kept an eye on her widowed father, Gustave, a local dairy farmer. She explained that her father was a steadfastly hard-working and honest man, though hardly a sociable one. Over the years, a protracted list of visiting, cap-in-hand pastors with all manner of pedigrees and strategies had failed to kindle Gustave's interest in church-related activities.

Gustave had grown up on the family farm and in the Catholic church. From there, he had traded his overalls for Army fatigues in the spring of 1942. Three years later, as VE Day approached, he returned to the farm with a pronounced disability. He dragged his left leg behind him wherever he went—brain damage inflicted by a sniper's bullet.

In 1950, Gustave had offered up an extensive, angry litany of decidedly unsanctimonious comments to heaven after his wife died during Isabelle's birth. Isabelle issued words of caution to Phil: "What's done is done."

A couple of weeks after hearing Isabelle's dissuading tale, Phil climbed into his car and resolutely headed to Gustave's dairy farm in order to pay a visit to the somber, reclusive farmer-father-veteran.

Phil made his unannounced, uninvited visit in the middle of an afternoon milking. The two men met near the barn door, and brief introductions ensued. "I have two dozen more full udders that need my attention," Gustave informed him. Phil watched as Gustave turned his back and laboriously limped to the impatiently waiting cows.

Preceding pastors who, in trepidation, had made their way to the farm had stopped at the barn door, perhaps shouting comments and invitations to the preoccupied Gustave. Phil stepped into the barn and followed his new acquaintance on his rounds. There was no mention of doctrine or creed, of grace or atonement. Phil listened as Gustave sang to his cows (in French) and called them by name. By the time the afternoon milking had come to an end, the farmer was smiling. Phil's dress shoes and neatly pressed pants featured newly accumulated layers of odiferous, all-natural, organic fertilizer.

"Come back another afternoon if you want," Gustave commented. "Sing with me. I do know a few songs in English, though my girls won't understand the words."

After that initial visit, Gustave found his way to an occasional church service where he would sit quietly with Isabelle. Phil returned to the cow barn for visits and became more acquainted with the milking process as well as the dispositions and vague peculiarities of each of Gustave's "girls." Phil's most cherished Christmas gift? His own pair of barn boots.

My thoughts: Meeting people where they are—without judgment, condition, or hesitation—how Christ-like is that? My first lesson gleaned from Gary's story fell in the realm of outreach. Subsequent reflections have focused on Phil's commitment and perseverance. Whether we are aware of it or not, our level of commitment is obvious to those around us. I confess to being easily sidetracked or discouraged. Frequently, I admit, I give up too easily and punt. This true story brings a weighty abundance of grist to my mill.

> *The Northeast Kingdom is a region of jumbled mountains, deep forests, glacial lakes, and scattered hill farms where people still live close to the world of nature that we were all once part of.*
>
> —Howard Frank Mosher

BERRY PICKING LICKING

In the autumn of 1989, I joined some friends for a camping weekend near Ripton, Vermont. Upon reaching our remote campsite, we pitched our tents, shared some s'mores, admired the full and fetching fall colors surrounding us, and then turned in for the night.

A cool, restful night's sleep awaited us—well, most of us. As I was to learn, my friend Liz had applied blueberry-flavored scented lip balm before zipping into her sleeping bag. A couple of hours later, she awoke to bad breath, snuffly snorting, and one raspy tongue. A wandering black bear had picked up the scent of blueberries.

Liz somehow remained motionless until the rough tongue had removed the last of the sweet-smelling balm. At that point, the bear turned tail and wandered back into the woods. Liz waited a minute or two, changed her underwear, and then gaspingly shared the details of her late-night visit with us. No one doubted her story. It was evident by the look on her "ursine clean" face that she spoke from experience.

> *When a pine needle falls in the forest, the eagle sees it;*
> *the deer hears it; the bear smells it.*
>
> —Iroquois Saying

SHEEP

In the mid-1990s, I worked as a youth leader at a church just south of Burlington, Vermont.

Steven, a member of my little collective, was a reserved, contemplative teenager who was less than enthralled with the day-to-day rigors of school. His dad was a dairy farmer, so Steven found solace in quiet life on the farm—and in church. Often I would look at Steven and find myself thinking, "Still waters run deep."

Steven's senior year of high school was vexing. The other seniors in the youth group were all making plans to head off to college. Steven kept silent on the topic, but those close to him were aware that he wanted nothing further to do with educational endeavors. One winter day, Steven came by for a visit. He informed me that he would be looking for a full-time job upon graduation and that he had made another decision: He wanted to be a volunteer fireman. When I asked how he had reached this particular decision, he responded, "I want to help people. If a guy's house is on fire, he won't care a bit if I never made the honor roll at school."

In those years, I lived out in the country and commuted 9 miles to work. I drove the same route to work every day and loved every inch of it—awe-inspiring views of Lake Champlain and (beyond) the imposing Adirondacks. Along the way, I would pass two dairy farms and one sheep farm.

One cool spring morning, I was driving to work just as dawn broke when I spotted red lights flashing in the distance. A line of fire trucks and pickups had parked along Irish Hill Road. The beacons cast an eerie glow across split-rail fences, outbuildings, and swaying birch trees. As I drew closer, I knew that something was very wrong.

There had been a fire in the sheep barn a few hours earlier. By the time I arrived, the fire had been extinguished. I spotted Steven's truck parked haphazardly, three wheels on the grass and one barely hanging onto the asphalt. Steven was a reluctant conversationalist, but folks could count on him to be there when things went south. This morning was no exception.

I pulled over and waited for Steven as a few men lingered near the smoking remains. As I soon learned, the firefighters had arrived promptly, and with the farmers pitching in, they had managed to get every single sheep out of the burning barn. But that's when the real battle began. In the confusion, some of the sheep, panicked and disoriented, tried to bolt back into the barn, the place they had long associated with safety. They couldn't grasp that their familiar haven was no longer safe. Farmers had called, coaxed, and pulled, but the panicked animals had struggled to comprehend. In the end, despite the best efforts of farmers and firefighters, about a third of the flock died.

That was Steven's third structure fire and his first with any sort of fatality. The impact was palpable. Steven shook his head, exhaled, and mournfully commented, "We had enough time."

After a couple of angst-ridden minutes, we both began thinking about the symbolism surrounding the morning's events. All the sheep knew the voice of the farmers. All the sheep knew the barn and what it represented. Some of the sheep had trusted the farmers above all else. Others had put their trust in the barn. Each animal had a choice to make, and survival weighed in the balance.

From time to time, I face similar decisions. Where do I place my trust in crises?

For where your treasure is, there your heart will be also.
—Matthew 6:21 (NIV)

GREEN MOUNTAIN MEMORY

In the mid-to-later 1990s, I was employed as a research technician at the University of Vermont's School of Natural Resources. I was beyond fortunate to spend my summers on Lake Champlain and my winters in the snow-stilled Green Mountains.

In this role, I utilized several modes of transportation: an ancient but dependable four-wheel-drive Chevy pickup, the University's 45-foot research vessel (the R/V Melosira), a snowmobile, an 18-foot Mako skiff, cross-country skis, and my big feet.

One February day, I was scheduled to check on some weather-monitoring equipment at the University's Green Mountain Research Forest near Wolcott, Vermont. Through the course of the preceding night, my house had received about 20 inches of snow. I knew from experience that the Wolcott area would likely have received twice that amount, all piled atop considerable accumulation from previous storms. Around sunrise, I went to check with my boss regarding plans for the day. Without saying a word, he handed me his pair of snowshoes and smiled a little smile.

My first thought was to reply, "I'm a North Carolina boy. I have no idea how to attach these things to my feet, much less put them to use." I thought better of it, took the worn, out-sized, cumbersome snowshoes, and muttered a half-hearted "thanks."

I retreated to the equipment room where I struggled with my boots and the leather straps of the snowshoes until I got the gist of it. After a heavy sigh, I threw the snowshoes into the truck's bed, along with my usual supplies and equipment, and headed out. As I drove eastward toward the mountains, I marveled at the newly fallen snow (because if you can't appreciate the beauty of Vermont's snow, you're doomed), all the while pondering and rejecting several strategies for the day. I was not foolhardy enough to expect smooth sailing.

With some effort and a bit of luck, I was able to get the truck to the entrance of the research forest. Unlocking the gate and driving the quarter mile to the tiny cabin was a summer, fall, and (sometimes) spring procedure. Winter visits would invariably involve trudging through snow. When I opened the truck door that morning, I was greeted by a 0 degree blast of air. Thankfully, I did have enough sense to pull on my insulated coveralls before fumbling through the shoeing process.

The task at hand: Relocate a 15-pound deep cycle battery (and other supplies) from the bed of the truck to a weather-monitoring station. The battery fit nicely into a type of pack-sling thingy that I would bind to my back. On a good day, carrying the battery was cumbersome. On that particular day, it meant that I had to adjust to my new, temporary center of gravity while . . . learning to walk.

I gazed up the slope toward my destination and was instantly puzzled and disoriented. Where was the gate? The tops of the posts on either side stood about 4 feet off the ground; they were nowhere to be seen. My thoughts turned to a quote from George Orwell: "This has become un-fun."

Let me pause now and say that learning to use snowshoes in 5 feet of snow is, I would imagine, like learning to weather Hollywood egos by spending five days in a life raft with Barbra Streisand.

The first thing I noticed after taking a few tentative steps was that snowshoes do not, in fact, allow you to walk on snow; they allow you to sink into it more slowly than you would otherwise. In very short order, I also learned that falling was pleasantly painless—even fun with plenty of soft snow on all sides to catch me. A ten-year-old boy could happily spend a morning doing just that. From my physics classes, I remembered the concept of stopping distance. Loads of stopping distance surrounded me. The dilemma proved to be in regaining an upright position.

After the first of countless tumbles, I felt like a turtle on its back. Certainly, the battery did not help. The ground, my long-trusted friend and reference point was maddeningly difficult to locate. I rested for a minute and gazed skyward. It was quite an interesting perspective. I remember thinking, "I am Timmy in the well. Only Lassie is home by the fireplace, serenely oblivious to my plight."

Thoughts of Lassie introduced a whole 'nother topic to my addled brain: animals. I considered all the animals and animal tracks I had seen in the vicinity—moose, black bears, coyotes, foxes, raccoons. The bears didn't concern me. They would be snoozing contentedly, dreaming raspberry-bush dreams. My eyes widened when I remembered another woodland creature, a relative of the wolverine, the animal my wildlife professor called a "skill saw with four legs." Imagine a wolverine with an ingrown toenail, an unsatisfying home life, and recently disconnected utilities. Of all the animals in the forest, the one I feared most was the fisher, 10 pounds soaking wet. With more than a smidge of trepidation, I recalled an autumn day when, unnervingly near my present location, I had disturbed a fisher standing guard over an eviscerated porcupine carcass. I had seen firsthand what the fisher was capable of.

From my studies, I remembered that in addition to porcupines, the fisher diet included rabbits, birds, rodents, and larger mammals, including deer. My thinking was that the fishers of Wolcott could, if given half a chance, add "incapacitated, flailing research technician" to this list. After briefly pondering this dismal fate, I willed myself back to vertical.

After each successive fall, I would thrash around like a fish in a waterless bucket until I had compacted enough snow to fashion a type of base. Off I would go for another 15 feet.

In a matter of a very few minutes, my heart was pounding out of my chest. My pulse raced, I gasped for air, and I became lightheaded. My coveralls had become my own private sweat lodge. Back in those days, I was in reasonably good shape. The task at hand would doubtlessly be fatal for me today.

In short order, I realized that the coveralls would have to go. That meant the snowshoes would have to come off, as well as my boots. To state the obvious, it was quite a dispiriting undertaking. The process was helped along by shouts and a myriad of other strange noises. Distant neighbors could be forgiven for assuming that hidden in the newly created crater were Björk and (Vermont's own) Howard Dean, engaged in a fight to the death. By the time I reached the weather-monitoring station, I had stripped down to a long-sleeved T-shirt and blue jeans.

I installed the new battery, checked the rest of the equipment at the site, and then stared down at the old battery that had been replaced. I knew it had to make its way back to Burlington that afternoon. If I had been flush with cash that day, I would have stopped at the South Burlington Sears on my way back to campus and purchased a brand-new battery, gladly leaving the old one behind for the fishers to eat.

> *On the sled, in the box, lay a third man whose toil was over, —a man whom the Wild had conquered and beaten down until he would never move nor struggle again.*
>
> —Jack London

UNCLE ONNA THAWS OUT

My Vermont winters? When the air was so cold it felt like my skin was being sandblasted, my first wife and I would grant ourselves annual reprieves: a week in Myrtle Beach. In addition to thawing out, I got to see my sister and her family, which meant I was also granted invaluable time with my nephew and niece. When those two spark plugs were toddlers, they had difficulty pronouncing the letter L. One casualty from this temporary difficulty was my name, so "Allen" became "Onna."

At the hotel pool and out on the beach, Onna tried his best to keep up with the dynamic duo, bouncing and splashing like someone auditioning for the role of Fun Uncle in a regional television commercial. This worked for about an hour, and then I would collapse into a semi-prone heap (half drowned, half comatose) and flip my internal switch from "Play" to "Observe and Report."

The children had their own toggle switches that cycled regularly between "inseparable best friends" and "mortal enemies who must be destroyed." The two switch positions were labeled

"Laugh" and "Kill." Adults in attendance were expected to track the switch positions at all times because we never knew when giggles in the shallow end might morph into carnage.

Whenever the toggle flipped to "Kill" mode, I would watch from my ringside seat as the parents of the combatants attempted to disentangle the pugilists. With each bout, Harvey Logan (from *Butch Cassidy and the Sundance Kid*) would provide the audio for my brain: "Rules? In a knife fight? No rules!"

I received continuing education credits in the strange and sticky world of child-rearing: sippy cups that could double as squirt guns, unwieldy car seats engineered by NASA, diaper changes that required HazMat suits, and *Fahrenheit 451* meltdowns. Add in horsey rides that unfailingly ended in rug burn, shrieks that could break glass, and more questions than I'd fielded during my college exams, and you have a fairly complete picture.

Still, the highlight was invariably the hotel's lazy river. For the kids, it meant endless hours of giggling, wiggling, and wet chaos. For me, it was the perfect metaphor: drifting, endlessly circling, occasionally capsizing, and never quite reaching the exit.

I encountered a multi-year cross-section of questions:

> "Why do you live so far away?"
>
> "Why don't you have kids?"
>
> "Why does that man only have one arm? I'm gonna go ask him."
>
> "Did they have cars when you were a boy?"
>
> "Why do you keep making me mad?"
>
> "Why do we have to go to bed? You are the one who's tired!"

"Dogs and cats don't have to wear clothes, but people do. Who makes up these rules?"

"Is Mama your mama too?" (Loved that one!)

From my niece's "Statement" category:

"An oncologist is a doctor who is always on call."

"My brudder said the 'F' word!" (Thinking that "fanny" was the "F" word.)

Each friend represents a world in us, a world possibly not born until they arrive, and it is only by this meeting that a new world is born.

—Anaïs Nin

AN INTERLUDE WITH SKATING ROYALTY

September 1996. The noon faculty and staff pickup basketball hour had just come to a merciful end at the University of Vermont's Patrick Gym. With a groan born from soreness, I grabbed my keys and water bottle and proceeded down the subterranean hallway to the men's locker room. Unbeknownst to me, the gym's steamy facility had been temporarily repurposed to accommodate shower-seekers from the connected hockey rink, a facility that had suffered a recent plumbing failure. As I approached, the locker room door swung open. A couple of New York Rangers strode confidently into the hallway.

An out-of-body realization ensued. I remembered reading something in the *Burlington Free Press* about the Rangers' use of the university's hockey rink for their pre-season training camp. I was, nonetheless, ill-prepared to encounter Wayne Gretzky and Brian Leetch. After rubbing elbows with the greatest hockey player in history not named Gordie Howe, I turned to find

Mark Messier and a few demi-gods gathering their belongings. (Ah, yes. A pause here in solemn remembrance of those days of yore when Mark and I both had hair to complement our determined jawlines.)

The abruptness was surreal. I had encountered famous people before, mostly in airports or places where the concentration of celebs was predictably higher (*e.g.*, Madison Avenue). These guys had seemingly gone out of their way to make cameos in my mundane routine. From my small-town perspective, this paralleled Don Drysdale's appearance in the backyard of the Brady Bunch.

On my walk home, the realization hit me: If I had excused myself from the last pickup game, I could have spent the remainder of my days claiming that I had once showered with Gretzky and Messier. The three of us, all born in 1961, reflecting on the 1,500+ goals we had (collectively) scored, who knows? Perhaps I could have joined them in "Hit Somebody (The Hockey Song)." [Note for the Chronology Police: Yes, I am aware that "Hit Somebody (The Hockey Song)" was not written or recorded until 2001. Here's the thing: my daydream, my rules.]

> *Hockey is the chance of life, and an affirmation that despite the deathly chill of winter we are alive.*
>
> —Stephen Leacook

LIFE ON EAST AVENUE

During my last couple of years in Vermont, I found myself surrounded by a preponderance of neighbors who defiantly marched to the beat of their own drums. One neighbor with a notably free-spirited cadence was Iris, a young woman who ran a health food store on Main Street. She was famous (infamous?) for her spontaneous, exuberant, late-night parties, including more than a few where she was the lone partier, banging on her ancient piano, much to the consternation of her housemates (Garrett, Stephon, and the rather high-strung Phoebe).

Late one summer evening, after Burlington had settled into its usual mid-week state of drowsy tranquility, a traveler by the name of Bob found himself with a pressing need for herbal relief. Bob wasn't after anything scandalous (nothing that would raise eyebrows at the church picnic), just a bottle of herbal medicine.

As fate would have it, the health food store was closed for the night, but Bob's after-hours phone call was forwarded to Iris' place. Iris, being the accommodating sort she was, answered the call. She assured him that she had a few containers of the remedy available at her home. If Bob was so inclined, he could swing by and save them both a trip to the store. Iris' East Avenue house was, after all, a mere mile from the store.

An appreciative Bob arrived a few minutes later. Iris greeted him at her front door and led him into the spacious living room. "Just sit tight," she exclaimed. "I'll grab it." And off she went, disappearing into the depths of the house like a character in one of those mystery novels that Iris herself was (perpetually) too distracted to open.

Left to his own devices, Bob did what anyone might do when seated near an unattended piano. He began picking out tunes, random bits of melody half-remembered and half-improvised, the sort of music that arises when a person isn't too worried about being heard.

Unfortunately for Bob, someone was listening.

Upstairs, Phoebe (who, mind you, was never what you'd call a morning person or, it seemed, much of an evening person) was rudely awakened by the unexpected clamor. She had retired sometime earlier, expecting nothing more than a peaceful night's rest, her face slathered in night cream. The exploratory notes from the piano wafted up the stairs to Phoebe's ears. Filled with a deep, unfiltered loathing that could only come from an untimely awakening, Phoebe arose.

She descended the staircase in her nocturnal glory, her feet snug in a pair of bunny slippers that, despite their innocent appearance, had seen more stomping than hopping. There was no question in her agitated mind; Iris would soon be on the receiving end of a withering tongue-lashing.

Phoebe turned the corner at the bottom of the stairs and opened her mouth to unleash her vitriol, only to find Bob, not Iris, at the piano—Bob Dylan, that is.

> *Anyone can become angry—that is easy, but to be angry with the right person and to the right degree and at the right time and for the right purpose, and in the right way—that is not within everyone's power and is not easy.*
>
> —Aristotle

MAPPING MY FUTURE

While working as a research technician at the university, I kept bill collectors at bay by riding what academics refer to as "the soft-money wave." I followed grant money (even rumors about grant money) around the building with a mixture of persistence and thinly veiled desperation. Within the constraints of funded projects, I gained valuable experience on several fronts: learning all manner of procedures, becoming more acquainted with scientific method, getting to know the departmental staff, calculating the professional and financial ebbs and flows, and cautiously navigating the stratified pecking order within the academic department (from departmental chair to the work-study students).

Throughout those years, I submitted applications for natural-resource positions all over the United States. By rough estimate, I mailed or e-mailed painstakingly constructed cover letters and applications for 250 positions. The fruits of my labors? Four interviews, a cascade of rejection letters, and scores of dead ends. Another period of uncertainty had reared its ugly head; my aspirations became imperiled.

Near the decade's end, I realized that the time had come to reassess my marketable skills and shift my career focus. In my coursework and within the aforementioned projects, I had become proficient with a new (at the time) type of software: geographic information systems (GIS). Mapping aspects of my project work included but were not limited to the processing and incorporation of field-collected spatial data.

And the charted path reached from my time spent in deliberation? I would reach back to the fascinations of my childhood where a well-thumbed atlas, a glove box overflowing with gas-station maps, and a depository of *National Geographic* magazines had hinted at mysteries untold. I would reinvent myself as a cartographer, a maker of maps. Can you hear the disembodied voice? "Recalculating."

> *That is the charm of the map. It represents the other side of the horizon where everything is possible.*
>
> —Rosita Forbes

PART 4:
CHARTING A NEW CAREER IN A NEW CENTURY (SUBURBAN RALEIGH AND BEYOND)

HENRY'S FOLLY

Seven coworkers and I recently descended on the seaside city of Savannah, Georgia, in order to update our map database for the area — "ground truthing." Due to the convenient fact that our hotel was located at the city's center (East Bay Street), Jane and I were able to enjoy a respite from serving as the team's designated drivers each night.

During the course of our second evening in the city, Henry (rather predictably) became the first of the assemblage of cartographers to self-medicate into that fuzzy realm beyond latitude and longitude. Not for the first time, Jane and I were keenly aware that it would take more than twenty-four GPS satellites to guide Henry back to his waypoint.

Late in the night, Jane and I did our level best to herd our six compromised friends back to the hotel. Despite these commendable best efforts, Henry lost orbit and ventured too close to the Yamacraw Bluff and 13 feet lower, the Savannah River. With a single high-pitched squeak, Henry dropped from view. Faint echoes of a splash followed.

Seven sets of eyes peered from the bluff down to the river's surface. Between gurgles, Henry communicated that he was okay but would not be averse to accepting a bit of assistance. As Henry scanned his aquatic environs for a means of egress, he focused on what in his disoriented state appeared to be a large wooden ladder.

While Emily and Peter scurried across the street in search of help, Henry struggled to reach and climb the wooden ladder. As the soggy events played out, we all bore witness to the inescapable reality that being fully clothed, impressively intoxicated, and locationally challenged would not turn out to be a recipe for successful ascension. With urgent flailing and a sailor's vocabulary, Henry climbed three rungs. As he paused to catch his breath, he was perplexed to find that only his head and shoulders were above water. With a burst of energy, Henry spurred himself upward. Another three rungs cleared. Inexplicably (to Henry), he remained waterlogged and very much at the river's surface. Near the end of his third ill-fated attempt to scale the ladder, help arrived in the form of a deckhand. The large wooden "ladder" Henry had been attempting to climb was actually the freely turning paddle wheel of a river boat. "You remind me of one of those little flappers on *Wheel of Fortune*," I shouted helpfully.

After Henry had been rescued from the river's depths, we did our best to dry him off (at least on the outside). Later in the week in a solemn ceremony, we updated the map database for the city with a new point of interest: "Henry's Folly." The reference point stayed in the database for more than five years before a soberly humorless administrator removed it.

> *Give a man a fish, and he will eat for a day. Teach him how to fish, and he will sit in a boat and drink beer all day.*
>
> —George Carlin

OLE AND LENA

Over the course of the first four years of the new century, I traveled to Fargo, North Dakota, once or twice a year for work-related meetings or training. One of the highlights (in winter, there were precious few) was the chance to listen to members of the local populace as they recited, with vestigial Norwegian accents, litanies of Ole and Lena jokes. The following (two-part) tale never fails to remind me of my dad.

So Ole is at home on his deathbed, and he whispers to Lena, "Is everyone here?" Lena replies, "Yes, Ole, we're all here: Ole Jr. and Henrik, Anders, your brother Oskar, your sister Linnea, your cousins Espen and Britta. We're all here, Ole." Ole looks around and says, "If you're all in here, why are the lights on in the living room?"

The following day, Ole feels a bit better. He shuffles to the kitchen and sees the freshly baked kransekake on the counter. Lena barks:

"Don't even think about it, Ole. That's for the funeral."

—Lena

GETTING SCHOOLED

I remember ACC basketball in its leaner days, a conference of seven schools, when its rhythms and rivalries were at once fierce and familial. The games carried an intimacy. Schools shared not just a conference but a story. Despite forty years of notable changes in collegiate basketball (within and without the conference), I jumped at a fortuitous opportunity to witness the North Carolina State men's team in action against the Virginia Cavaliers.

Quite unexpectedly, a friend of similar age and inclination had received a couple of tickets that very afternoon. As it turned out, I was Roger's third choice to be his companion for the night. His wife was uninterested, and their thirteen-year-old son was sidelined with a sore throat ("DNP" in basketball parlance). I perceived no slight as I took in this bit of news. "Glad to go! I can come by and pick you up."

When I arrived at Roger's house, he rushed from his front door and made it halfway down the front walkway. "Ah! The tickets! We might need those." As he turned to head back to the house, I asked him to wait up as my bladder was clambering for attention.

Roger pointed to the bathroom and then went up to his bedroom to retrieve the forgotten tickets. After a moment of welcomed relief, I headed back to the front door, only to pause and take notice of Sandra and Rupert (respectively Roger's wife and son) perched on the largest sofa sectional I had ever seen. On the much-cited spectrum of "multiple-butt furniture," Roger's sectional sits (ahem) at the opposite end of the aforementioned spectrum from Arlo Guthrie's "Group W Bench." The entire NCSU team could comfortably relax on the sectional and watch while Roger and I attempted to slow down the Virginia squad with a 1-1-0 zone defense.

Along with echoes from Roger's upstairs toilet flush, I overheard snippets of a rather one-sided conversation between mother and eighth-grade son. The two were occupying 1/20th of the sectional as they perused the boy's school yearbook. I couldn't help but notice that the mother held a pencil in her hand. Sandra, in turn, noticed my curiosity. "Rupert has expressed an interest in dating. This is a new development. I'm helping him narrow his possibilities." Rupert, for his part, looked stricken, his face a silent plea: "Save me."

Sandra continued with her unsolicited assistance in The Great Winnowing. Girl by girl, the photos of Rupert's classmates awaited judgment from the sharp point of Sandra's pencil. Rupert: "What about her? She's nice." Sandra: "With a nose like that, she has to be." It was an absurd and tragic exchange, an unvarnished glimpse into the mechanics of misguided maternal strategy. I took my leave before the conversation could veer further into the bizarre.

Roger talked about sports on our way to the game, but my mind lingered on Sandra's unabashed efforts to steer her son toward his thin, flawlessly complexioned, and high-cheek-boned classmates. The more I reflected, the more tawdry Sandra's *modus operandi* became. I thought of Rupert's ten-year-old sister. I could envision her as she retrieved an ice cream sandwich from the freezer, only to return it as she absorbed her mother's running commentary.

After the game, I thanked Roger as I dropped him off at his house. As is my habit, I waited long enough to ensure that he found his way through the front door. After Roger extinguished the porch light, I drove a mile to a deserted parking lot and stopped for additional pondering. I reminded myself of a simple truth: Every family, in its own way, is dysfunctional.

> *People talk about dysfunctional families. I've never seen any other kind.*
>
> —Sue Grafton

FERNWEH

Fernweh: noun. German. The pain of not being in foreign lands. A desire for travel. An ache for distant places.

My employer provided the balm for three-and-a-half years to ease my fernweh. I threw caution to the wind, shifted gears, and joined the newly created international team. Over this dizzying span of time, I visited twenty-eight countries on five continents (in addition to tantalizingly brief stops at airports in Rome, Reykjavik, Seoul, Mumbai, and Paris. At one point, it became necessary to return my passport to the State Department so fresh pages could be added. For the years 2004 and 2005, I was out of the United States for more days than I was in. I didn't just embrace travel; I marinated in it.

Those three-and-a-half years were immensely enjoyable as I eagerly adjusted to globe-trotter mode. As I began my fourth year, I realized that as much as I reveled in waking to greet new days in exotic, far-flung locales, I was simultaneously burning out on travel. The rewarding, gratifying experience was exhausting me.

The international team's standard trip length was three to four weeks, long enough to settle into the culture I was visiting.

My good-natured and industrious coworkers hailed from the United States, Sweden, Brazil, England, Mexico, France, Germany, Croatia, Spain, Canada, and Finland. Teams were assigned for each project, with the selection of members based on availability, geographic proximity, language skills, driving experience (driving on the left or right), and for destinations like Saudi Arabia, gender.

Some of the mapping projects focused on large cities. Other projects were concerned with networks of interconnected highways. Nearly half of the projects were a mix of the two. Each team member would be driven by a local driver for city projects. For highway projects, team members would (usually) be paired up. I enjoyed meeting and working with the local drivers but preferred the highway projects. Large cities the world over have a certain sameness. The character of a country is, at least for me, more readily identifiable in towns and in the countryside.

The ensuing pages are comprised of a couple of dozen "letters home" that have survived the years. Other letters and writings have, over time, disappeared during moves and/or with the introduction of new computer hardware and software.

> *Though we travel the world over to find the beautiful,*
> *we must carry it with us, or we find it not.*
>
> —Ralph Waldo Emerson

DESERT DAYS

Greetings from Oman!

I am road-weary but otherwise in good shape. Seven coworkers and I had initially been tasked with mapping the 2,500-year-old city of Muscat but have since been dispersed throughout the country like so many maple tree whirligigs. Some random thoughts and observations follow (sorry if I bounce around).

The Islamic culture is, of course, very different, and I try my best not to do anything to offend the agreeable folks. I have yet to meet an unfriendly or rude Omani. To date, I have seen or heard very little in the way of anti-Western sentiment. The government-run newspapers that I peruse reflect an anti-Israeli bent but nothing inflammatory or caustic. On most days, Sultan Qaboos delivers a brief note of greetings to his people.

Yesterday, Ishti (my driver) and I stopped at a promising restaurant in downtown Sinaw. We selected a table that overlooked the produce market (*souq*) and then hungrily looked at our menus. To my chagrin, there were no accompanying pictures for the variety of entrees, so I asked Ishti to interpret and also provide suggestions. When the aproned proprietor arrived at our table, he caught a bit of our discussion. "You American?" I replied that I was, indeed. He smiled and announced (in broken English), "You, first American here, my restaurant! You no pay food today." I grinned at him with an appreciative feeling of camaraderie, along with a flicker of pride at my bit of off-the-beaten-path adventure.

Today was yet another long, hot day of driving beneath the unrelenting sun. At the end of our work day, Ishti invited me to visit his house. Such impromptu invites had been a semi-regular occurrence for a few of my coworkers but a first for me. Hot tea or coffee held zero appeal for me, especially in triple-degree weather. Thankfully, I had been informed by a seasoned coworker that refusing the offer of food or drinks at a host's home is considered insulting and rude in Oman (and indeed elsewhere on the Arabian Peninsula). Thus, I accepted a cup of tea and sat down to meet Ishti's curious sons, ages six and three. The industrial-strength tea delivered a mule's kick, and I struggled to keep my eyes in their sockets. The boys, distracted from their afternoon play, seemed amused.

As I meander through life, hopping from one side of the globe to the other, there's something wonderfully heartening about the fact that children, bless their little souls, are simply children, no matter where you are. There's no need for a translator when it comes to understanding the universal chaos of kids. They tumble over one another, laughing at jokes only they seem to understand. The secret language of childhood transcends culture. And a mother's love—whether in the frantic hustle of a big city or the quiet solitude of a distant hamlet—is as constant and reassuring as the passage of time itself. It's one of those comforting truths that makes you feel a little better about the world.

Omani teenagers have proven to be an intriguing spectacle. Within a culture where boys and girls attend separate schools, pray in separate spaces, and are generally not permitted to mix in public, we might suppose that those limitations would put a damper on teenage flirtation. Ah, but teenagers are tirelessly resourceful. In the bustling souqs of the cities, for instance, I have spotted girls strolling along with their phone numbers scribbled discreetly on the palms of their hands. Should an interesting boy catch a girl's eye, all she had to do was wave. If the feeling is mutual, it's not long before they're deep in conversation—on their phones, of course, because why let a little thing like cultural norms get in the way of youthful curiosity?

Beyond the reaches of the city of Muscat, the landscape is barren: hills, scrubby plants, and sand, with mountains in the background. Radio stations are rare, and the kilometers can be monotonous. The towns in central Oman are few and far between. As a result, many of the people in this region live rather nomadic lives. Modern conveniences are scarce.

Even within the city of Muscat (the only sizable city in Oman), modern technology is a comparatively recent phenomenon. Oil was discovered here at a later date than in surrounding countries, so the influx of oil money is markedly more recent. As late as 1970, there were no paved roads in the country. (Note: A deluge of changes arrived in 1970 when the more progressive Sultan Qaboos took the reins.) At that time, literacy rates were around 30 percent, and very few Omanis had electricity, indoor plumbing, and so on.

We can ponder the merits of the sudden changes brought about by oil money (or money in general), but one clearly positive aspect can be seen in the building of schools and the rise in the literacy rate (now up to an estimated 65 percent). I pause to think of the young children attending school now. A generation ago, they would have spent their days tending herds of goats or carrying water to their villages.

The influence of Islam is all-encompassing. Nothing quite compares to the sound of Muslims being called to prayer, especially in small towns where the calls are amplified only by ancient wooden megaphones. The crime rate there is among the lowest in the world, and neighbors have a very dim view of troublemakers. Tradition holds sway. Admittedly, for Omani women, career choices, education, and clothing are very limited. The lot of women there appears to be improving, although not rapidly. Westerners have very little interaction with Omani women, basically none outside of Muscat.

Sultan Qaboos and his government run practically everything, from utilities to car dealerships to office buildings. Omanis do not have opportunities to vote, but all-in-all they seem happy and friendly. I am doing my best to follow suit.

> *I was highly pleased and full of those little pulses of excitement that come with finding yourself in a new place. I can't think of anything that excites a greater sense of childlike wonder than to be in a country where you are ignorant of almost everything. Suddenly, you*

are five years old again. You can't read anything, you have only the most rudimentary sense of how things work, you can't even reliably cross a street without endangering your life. Your whole existence becomes a series of interesting guesses.

—Bill Bryson

SWEDEN AND DENMARK

On an enjoyable interlude on my trip home from the Middle East, I awoke in a bunkbed aboard a retired (and stationary) Swedish cruise ship (the M/S *Rygerfjord*) and decided to kick the new day off by scrubbing in an expansive, sunlit shower room. The captain's bridge had been converted to a communal shower room for the ship's male guests. The gleaming room featured 180 degrees of windows (beginning at waist height) and overlooked both McLaren Bay and the Stockholm skyline. Stunning! Unequivocally, I can state that this was my first (and, in all likelihood, my last) opportunity to wave to a tugboat crew as I shampooed my hair.

After breakfast, Anne, my Adopted Sister and Amiable Traveling Companion (hereafter referred to as "ASATC Anne"), and I left the *Rygerfjord* and ambled across the Centralbran Bridge to the cavernous Stockholm Central Train Station. It is such a European thing to find that even the busiest bridges have been designed with pedestrians and cyclists in mind.

The five-plus hour train ride to Copenhagen is a breathtaking (and highly recommended) way to see rural Sweden. On our

Designated Rail Day morning, we caught glimpses of sleepy fishing villages along the Baltic Sea coast. Farther down the tracks, we found ourselves surrounded by endless Norway spruce and Scots pine forests, interspersed with picture-postcard towns. We were blessed with peeks into the lives of families who, by happy coincidence, were able to call the towns home. I smile now as I recall glowing images of tall, rosy-cheeked, self-assured Swedes—resplendent in their rugged, outdoorsy summer clothes—piling winsome, towheaded children into waiting Volvos.

All of this brought to mind Robert Frost's train-inspired "A Passing Glimpse": "Was something brushed across my mind that no one on earth will ever find? Heaven gives it glimpses only to those not in position to look too close."

We glided into Copenhagen's Central Rail Station in the still-sunny early evening. For a few hypnotic moments, we stood and watched the expansive "Departures" sign and reveled at the mesmerizing, mechanical clickity-clickity-clickity updates. City name after city name beckoned us like so many rectangular sirens: Milan, Amsterdam, Hamburg, Innsbrook, Nice, Sofia, Lisbon.

After this bit of daydreaming, we stepped out of the bustling station and danced or dodged our way through the phalanx of cyclists humming along the city streets. After several near-collisions, we arrived at our hotel where we dumped our packs and rather predictably headed off to the most touristy destination in Copenhagen: the Little Mermaid statue (although there was a slight delay involving a kiosk overflowing with German chocolates).

The whole world is a series of miracles, but we're so used to them that we call them ordinary things.

—Hans Christian Andersen,
Denmark's favorite son

GULF AIR

On my second trip to the Arabian Peninsula, I found myself learning far more than I had expected—less from the books I'd brought along and more from a contemplative awareness of Being There (not unlike Chance the Gardner). Before joining the international team, I had burdened myself with the usual Western assumptions, wrongly assuming that the cultures of the seven countries on the peninsula would be more or less interchangeable. After all, they're all clumped together on a map, right? But during my first two weeks back in Oman, I started to grasp not only the sheer size of the place (it is, after all, the largest peninsula in the world) but also the dizzying variety of subcultures that thrive both between and within these countries. For instance, life in the Dhofar Mountains of Oman is vastly different from life in the fishing villages that dot the Gulf of Oman and the Arabian Sea, even though you can reach them in the same afternoon (if you're willing to tackle a few terrifying mountain roads).

Then there's Yemen, the one country that remains firmly off limits to my team. How can I describe Yemen? If you cast the Arabian Peninsula countries as characters from *The Simpsons*, Yemen would undoubtedly be Nelson Muntz—surly, unpredictable, and always ready to deliver a punch.

Yesterday, after two enlightening weeks in Oman, I packed my bags for Bahrain. I boarded a Gulf Air flight from Muscat to Al Muharraq where I was to meet up with some coworkers and assist them with an ongoing mapping project. Boarding the plane involved a classic bit of travel nostalgia: walking across the tarmac and climbing the stairs as if I were flying off on a glamorous adventure with Gregory Peck and Ingrid Bergman.

It hit me as I began to make my way down the plane's aisle. This was anything but a typical Western business-class crowd. In fact, as I looked around, I realized I was the only Western person on the entire flight. That, of course, wasn't a problem . . . until it was.

As I took my seat, I could feel the eyes of nearly every passenger on the plane as they rested on me—not in an "Oh, look, a tourist" kind of way but in a "What is this guy doing on our plane?" kind of way. Curiosity, yes, but also pensiveness, distrust, and maybe a little fear—and not subtle either. No furtive glances here. They were sizing me up as if I were a headline from the evening news. I was a walking red flag. For the next ninety minutes, I was under surveillance. Mothers held their children a little closer, businessmen kept their eyes glued on me, and elderly couples exchanged quiet words of concern. Gregory Peck? Hardly. I was Peter Lorre.

And there it was: the cultural shoe firmly on the other foot. In their eyes, I was the potential threat. The anxious looks didn't let up until we touched down in Bahrain.

What stuck with me more than anything was the gift that flight had given me: a sharp and unexpected lesson in perspective. For a brief time, I got a taste of what it feels like to be the one who triggers suspicion simply by being there. And that's something I certainly could not have learned from a book or a briefing. It's the kind of experience that in the best way possible left me feeling a little smaller, a little more humbled, and immeasurably more aware of the world around me.

We don't see things as they are, we see them as we are.

—Anaïs Nin

BARCELONA

I flew from the Dubai airport to Barcelona at the end of the project. It was time to explore the Spanish Mediterranean coast while catching up with ASATC Anne (popping down from her home in Ireland). We had arranged a rendezvous at a train station near the bustling tourist information center. The ill-conceived plan was to amble up to the counter and ask for a few hotel/hostel recommendations. After all, it was September. Tourist season had come and gone.

Our first hint that our "plan" was quite possibly the worst plan since perching Michael Dukakis in the turret of a tank was the ever-lengthening line of tourists. We encountered a serpentine queue of road-weary travelers studying their guides and scratching their heads. (Head-scratching needs no translation.) After forty-five minutes, we made it to the counter where a cheery yet apologetic young woman informed us that there was no room in the inn.

We walked the surrounding area for another hour, investigating hotel and hostel lobbies, only to be met by shaking heads. Again, there was no interpretation needed. By that time, I had begun to contemplate a night of sleeping on the beach. At last, one sympathetic doorman suggested that we try heading south along the coast to check out some nearby communities that featured a few off-the-beaten-track hotels and bed and breakfasts.

Back to the train station, we lethargically boarded a sleek, two-level train and disembarked to the south—to the sleepy, beachy town of Sitges. Our luck changed at the third hotel, a tiny family-owned establishment with a dozen or so rooms. The proprietor proudly informed us that he had available rooms. "*¡Excelente!*" we replied with dramatic sighs of relief.

We spent three days exploring the beaches of Sitges and returning to Barcelona by day in order to see the sights, making sure to check out as many Antoni Gaudí buildings as time would allow. Prior to this trip, my favorite architect had been Frank Lloyd Wright. Ever after, it would be Gaudí. If Dr. Seuss had been an architect, he would have been Gaudí. We especially enjoyed La Sagrada Familia Cathedral and the Gaudí Museum at Park Güell.

As far as Sitges, we did enjoy the beaches, but we soon learned that after nightfall, Sitges was anything but sleepy. In Spain, it would seem, there is a perpetual succession of national festivals—festivals involving parades, horses, singing, drinking, castanets, blaring trumpets, booming fireworks, frenetic dancing—into the wee hours of the mornings. I believe the celebrations held during the course of our stay honored "The Great Festival of the Remembrance of the Day Armando's Terrier Decided to Leap from the Rooftop, Only to Think Better of It."

On the last morning, we went for one final swim, climbed aboard the train to the Barcelona airport, and then ventured onward to our respective homes in North Carolina and Dublin.

I now find myself suspended over the Atlantic Ocean, pondering the events of the past month and marveling at how travel seems to intensify images and memories.

> *I love Glasgow, but that love has always been matched with an urge to leave, to see over the horizon. And that pull has made me a proud citizen of the world.*
>
> —Billy Connelly

MEMORIES WITH MARTA AND KARLO

During my years with the international team, one particular undertaking stands out as a favorite: driving and mapping South Africa's national routes (the country's equivalent to our own interstate system). Five two-person teams drove the eastern half of the country's national routes for a memorable month-long project. Each weekend, we would rendezvous, divvy up remaining territories, and switch partners.

Each rented vehicle contained all manner of mapping hardware, a first-aid kit, a cell phone, a reference atlas, and a AAA guide to the country's many bed and breakfasts. Overnight stays in cities with hotels were reserved for team meet-ups. On a typical day, we would drive until sundown and then head to the nearest B&B in De Aar, Potchefstroom, Klerksdorp, Ladysmith, Polokwane, Welkom, Newcastle, Kroonstad, Mbombela, Richards Bay, Port Elizabeth, or Bethlehem. The names leap to mind in quick succession, even after fifteen years out of the country. And there were weekend cities: Kimberly, Johannesburg, Durban, Pretoria, Bloemfontein, and East London.

In the midst of this month of travel, Martin (my Swedish boss) and I spent two nights at a B&B in Pietermaritzburg, my favorite small city in all of South Africa. Nocturnal activities regularly included parking the car and heading out for long walks (if deemed safe), trying local restaurants (if available), and getting to know the hosts. Pietermaritzburg was no exception.

We stayed in a rambling, historic, two-story brick house that was surrounded by, of all things, eastern cottonwoods (decidedly non-native). Our preoccupied hostess chatted with us briefly when we checked in at the front desk. After that initial encounter, all our staff interactions were with the facility's caretakers, Karlo and Marta.

Marta helped us settle into our respective rooms while Karlo excused himself to retrieve our suitcases. When we returned from our nightly walk, we joined Karlo and two vacationing Scots in the living room where we began a friendly question-and-answer session. In short order, we learned that Karlo and Marta were brother and sister. They were also Croatian refugees. "We are all that we have in this world," Karlo said. As if on cue, Marta appeared near the end of this pronouncement. She and her older brother exchanged a brief glance that bore witness to their enduring bond.

Marta offered, "We are the two survivors. Everyone else is gone. Brothers, sisters, parents, aunts, uncles. Our father paid a king's ransom to get us aboard a fishing boat to Trieste. From there, we stowed away on a container ship, having no idea where it might be going. What's that English phrase? 'Any port in a storm?' As it turned out, the port was Durban." She went on to describe jumping from the ship at the mouth of the Durban harbor as she and Karlo utilized empty paint buckets as flotation devices.

The siblings had been in South Africa for seven years and in Pietermaritzburg for five. "Our jobs help us develop our language skills. We have much to be grateful for," Marta declared.

On the second night, we asked Karlo and Marta to join us for dinner and a walk. They agreed to meet up with us on our walk. Upon our return to the B&B, the four of us sat and talked late into the night. Karlo offered to show Martin and me their spartan basement bedroom as "the evening wore on" (to borrow a phrase from Elwood P. Dowd), a room with twin beds with a nightstand in between.

"We don't like to be apart, especially at night," Marta shared. Martin and I nodded our solemn understanding. "We do want to remember Croatia. We want to honor our family. We want to supplant memories of atrocities with earlier memories of growing up in our homeland."

Tacked to the wall just above the nightstand was a poem by Croatia's Drago Stambuk. Karlo translated for us.

> *Here are the pulses of the sea and the hands of love; Trembling, the blue Adriatic, and the billowing Ionian connect in the knot of indestructible union, under the crown of their inheritance they flow into the high seas. In Otranto, the lips coincide and the Croatian spirit sets its sails.*

COLOGNE, GERMANY

For our summer vacation, my first wife and I took advantage of her airline-employee status to visit her Oma (grandmother) in Cologne. In the course of one sunny afternoon, we made our way to Schildergasse, the epicenter of Cologne's shopping and fashion district.

After a tasty (though, for me, unpronounceable) lunch, we split up for an hour of "his and hers" shopping. Thus, I found myself strolling through the district alone when an anatomically gifted young woman approached me with an excited, distraught tone in her voice. She emphatically pleaded with me in German as she frenetically pointed at the window of a nearby store. Of course, I had no idea what the desperate woman was attempting to convey or why she happened to consider me, of all people, to be her only hope (her Obi-Wan Kenobi) for deliverance. In her state of urgent agitation, she pressed an out-sized womanly appendage against my bare arm and pleadingly pointed to her watch. As this woman's actions commanded (at a bare minimum) 100 percent of my attention, I presented no challenge for her accomplice who deftly breezed behind to relieve me of my wallet.

To do two things at once is to do neither.
—Publilius Syrus

KOWLOON / HONG KONG

Man, do I feel *tall*! —a feeling of power that is offset by the fact that I can't stand up in my shower or shop for clothes in my size. In addition, I have to avoid bopping the hotel sprinkler heads with my noggin, thereby setting off an indoor downpour.

My driver, Ivan, has proven to be more than adept at conversational English. He is a conscientious worker but likes to take a fifteen-minute break each morning and afternoon. He will pull off the road and (in less than a minute) be fast asleep. I busy myself with note-taking and then wake him when break time is over. Driving here is serious business with a maze of highways and intersections of dumbfounding complexity. I have to tell Ivan, "Right, then left . . . no left *here*, then right," all with urgent, panicky hand gestures. Occupants of passing cars must surely be convinced that I am experiencing seizures. At any rate, Ivan and I seem to be approaching something akin to a system (after four days).

Yesterday, as we found ourselves mired in the perpetual logjam of traffic on Nathan Road, Ivan pointed to a hotel on our right. "There is where the old Princess Theater stood." He turned to smile at me. "My older brother used to work as an usher there. He got me in to see the Beatles back in 1964. Well, no Ringo. But the other three were there." I considered this novel bit of news. Ivan had witnessed a rarity of rarities. That summer, Ringo had been fighting tonsillitis and was temporarily replaced by session drummer Jimmie Nicol. For a moment, I was lost in thought until Ivan abruptly brought me back to the present with a string of expletives directed at a taxi driver.

Hong Kong is a stunning city, or so I'm told. Actually, seeing it is a bit of a trick. This place wears fog and haze like a parka, so any sweeping view of the skyline has been, so far, impossible. But we live in hope. Perhaps one gloriously clear day we'll make it up to Victoria Peak to finally get that postcard-perfect view of the harbor.

On foggy mornings, Hong Kong could pass for a distant cousin of San Francisco with its mist-covered hills, choppy waters, and relentless activity. At other times, the city seems to transform itself into Stockholm with dozens of islands, endless shorelines, and ferries darting about as if they're late for something terribly important. It's all very disorienting. But then there are imposing mountains to the north that make it clear I'm in a city like no other.

The harbor itself is a veritable buffet of boats with traditional junks mingling alongside ferries, container ships, and tugboats, all weaving past each other in a surprisingly graceful aquatic ballet. It's a place where the old and the new seem to coexist in some unspoken truce. Even in this thoroughly modern city, bamboo scaffolding still embraces skyscraper construction, with men and women perched high above the streets, sometimes barefoot, clinging to the bamboo like acrobats. When I marveled at their audacity, my driver assured me that falls are remarkably rare and that they usually occur "during the monsoon season." Oh, okay. Let's add *that* into the mix!

My efforts to learn about the culture of Hong Kong continue. In the Middle East, it is "culturally correct" to use your right hand when offering or taking something. In Botswana, placing your left hand on the other person's right forearm during a handshake conveys respect. Similarly, in Hong Kong (and mainland China), the use of both hands in the midst of interpersonal exchanges demonstrates respect (and also that you are not hiding something with the other hand).

Appreciation and reverence for the elderly are paramount to Asian cultures, and Hong Kong is certainly no exception. A group of senior citizens meets in a courtyard outside my hotel window every morning at 7:00 for tai chi. I am absolutely fascinated by their dedication and concentration, to say nothing of their flexibility. At first, my thoughts were, "These people are working hard to stay active." Later, I realized that taking care of their bodies was and has been a lifelong endeavor. Food for thought for yours truly!

I am duly impressed with the Hong Kong YMCA. It is near my hotel, so I stopped in to take a look during last night's walk. Founded around 150 years ago, it is absolutely the embodiment of what a YMCA should be. The number and scope of the programs for the community is astonishing—daycare, senior care, all sorts of rehab, job-life skills for reforming prostitutes, physical fitness programs, prosthetic device fittings and training, language classes (including sign language), nutrition programs, prenatal care, suicide awareness and prevention training, and anything else worthwhile that you could imagine. The week's list of classes and programs covered a wall the size of a South of the Border billboard.

> *Life in Hong Kong transcends cultural and culinary borders, such that nothing is truly foreign and nothing that doesn't belong.*
>
> —Peter Jon Lindberg

MACAU

Geography Quiz:

What is the oldest European settlement in Asia? (answer: Macau)

Okay, where and what is Macau?

Like Hong Kong, Macau is a "special administrative area" of China. Macau sits on the south bank at the mouth of the Pearl River (with Hong Kong occupying the north side). Portugal governed Macau for almost 450 years before handing Macau back to China in 1999. The three small islands that comprise Macau now have 450,000 people living within their 9 square miles, so Macau is one of the most densely populated cities in the world.

Macau is a fifty-minute ferry ride from neighboring Hong Kong. Certainly, there are noteworthy parallels between Hong Kong and Macau, and at least as many differences. Despite a long Portuguese heritage, only 1,000 of the residents are ethnically Portuguese. Although Portuguese and Mandarin remain the two official languages of Macau, few folks here are fluent in Portuguese. However, Portuguese architecture is still on display in the majority of older public buildings. In Hong Kong, you can meet a friend for tea on the corner of Oxford Road and Yorkshire Street. In Macau, you can meet a friend for *sopa da casa* on the corner of Rua da Padre Antonio and Avienda de Paia Grande.

Macau, as it turns out, is a place that likes to keep its streets snug. Even the busiest streets are relatively narrow passageways between tall buildings. As you might imagine, that presents certain logistical challenges for those of us attempting to navigate with modern technology. Our GPS antenna, a device normally quite adept at knowing where it is in the world, found itself hopelessly befuddled as distorted signals bounced off the canyon-like walls of the city's skyscrapers.

But where technology faltered, good old-fashioned footwork prevailed. Armed with aerial photographs and a sense of adventure (or at least stubborn determination), the six of us took to the streets, one step at a time. And so we walked. And walked. And walked some more, covering kilometers of Macau's bustling core, dodging scooters, sidestepping delivery carts, and encountering all sorts of interesting characters along the way. It was, in many ways, the best possible way to experience life in the heart of the city.

On the whole, people were very curious, and most were quite helpful. "My" area was filled with a variety of machine shops, tiny restaurants, and open-air produce markets. As I walked along the sidewalks, I quickly learned to watch out for vats of boiling vegetable oil, acetylene torches, shards of flying metal, and other hazards. People working in the shops and restaurants have a penchant for using the sidewalks as work surfaces. Here are my two working theories: (1) the sidewalks are cooler, and (2) the sidewalk workers are able to see what is going on in their neighborhoods. I must admit that I often wondered what OSHA and state health inspectors would have said if they had been "along for the ride."

In Macau, as in Hong Kong, we noticed older residents taking their caged birds for outings in the local parks. All sorts of colorful (and noisy) birds were frequent visitors in the shady city parks. Owners take their birds to parks to provide them with opportunities to take in the sights, sounds, and smells of urban oases. Dogs and doggie parks in both cities are also plentiful. There are a lot of Corgis and Bulldogs in Hong Kong; Shar Peis in Macau.

The scooter is the undisputed vehicle of choice throughout Macau. In Hong Kong and Macau, folks in cars drive on the left side of the road. (Mainland China drives on the right to make things interesting and keep folks on their toes.) Scooters follow the path of least resistance and seem to be free from any laws or regulations. Before stepping off the curb, I have learned to look right for cars and look left and right for scooters. Luckily for me, the scooters here are exceedingly loud, so pedestrians do have warnings. The taxi drivers of Macau have the same loathing for scooters that my old boat captain (on Lake Champlain) has for jet skis.

One thing that never fails to amuse (and at times baffle) me is noticing which bits of Western culture have hitchhiked their way around the globe. No matter where I am, there are a few constants in cities. There's usually a 7-Eleven around the block, a KFC within reach, and throngs of people sporting Disney merchandise. Winnie-the-Pooh and Ariel seem to have made themselves at home in every part of the planet, which raises the question of whether they might be the most-traveled beings in human history.

In Hong Kong and Macau, however, Western culture takes on a particularly, shall we say, nostalgic twist. I was ill-prepared for the soundtrack of 1970s soft rock that wafts through every public space like a clingy perfume. Bread, America, Tony Orlando and Dawn, Captain & Tennille, Three Dog Night—they're all omnipresent here, serenading shoppers and pedestrians alike. I'd wager that any one of those bands could sell out stadiums in Hong Kong or Macau. An enterprising soul with blond hair and a pair of wire-rimmed glasses could market himself as "Howard, the John Denver Experience" and achieve local hero status.

Lots of songs I thought or hoped I would never hear again are now (once more) stuck in my head. I will do you the favor of failing to mention them by name.

Macau and Hong Kong continue to make the most of a truly wonderous natural harbor with a staggering amount of commerce. Due to their "special administrative" status, they are part of China but are unencumbered by Chinese import-export headaches. Basically, they function as a duopoly for the majority of Chinese trade. People come to this region to shop, find work, gamble, and make deals—big deals. After three weeks here, the scale is just beginning to dawn on me.

One day last year in the middle of the Omani desert, I heard a DJ ask listeners to name the river that formed the Grand Canyon. He would give a small prize. In the blink of an eye, a listener called with the correct answer (the Colorado River).

Yesterday, a local man in Macau asked me where my home was. I replied, "the United States." When he asked what part, I replied, "the South, near Florida." "Georgia, Carolinas?" he continued. When he learned that I was from North Carolina, he held up his pack of cigarettes and smiled. "You have tobacco fields there, but also beaches as well as some mountains." As I travel, I am so often reminded of how much people in other cultures know about us and how little we know about other cultures worldwide. This notion can leave us feeling tremendously self-important or red-faced at our own ignorance. I am hoping for the latter.

> *We must learn about other cultures in order to understand, in order to love, and in order to preserve our common world heritage.*
>
> —Yo-Yo Ma

EVERYONE IS HELPFUL, EVERYONE IS SO KIND ON THE ROAD TO ZABALA

For our first week in Uruguay, my coworkers and I patronized an agreeable hotel situated across the street from one of Montevideo's many comely city parks (Plaza Zabala). The hotel provided us with generous breakfasts on an elevated, streetside patio.

Breakfast has long been my favorite meal of the day, and the offerings provided by the hotel did not disappoint. Along with the delicious food, our dawns were enhanced by sights, sounds, and flowery fragrances from Plaza Zabala. During each morning of our stay, a trio of teen boys faced our hotel and graciously provided a gently swaying soundtrack that reflected the local culture. The trio of buskers was comprised of two baby-faced guitar players and one perpetually grinning marimba player. Their clothes, shoes, instruments, and even jaunty hats were worn and faded. Despite their appearance, or perhaps (in part) because of their appearance, their musical and vocal talents belied their age and enthralled passersby.

We were enamored with their musical selections and made a point of overtipping the boys (with pesos and food). On our third morning, Miguel and I spent a few interrupting minutes learning a bit more about the performers and their backstories. First, we discovered that the trio was comprised of two brothers and one cousin (my reaction? "Uruguayan Beach Boys!"). They all attended the local high school but spent time before and after school earning money for their appreciative families. The majority of their selections were traditional Uruguayan folk songs, but the boys mixed in obligatory snippets of pop (English and Spanish lyrics). Personal favorites were Tracy Chapman's "Fast Car" and an exuberant rendition of Lindsey Buckingham's "Holiday Road."

For six mornings in a row, the boys assumed their positions and then immersed themselves in thoughtfully considered melodies while simultaneously acknowledging the undulating migration of happenstance audience members. The world that surrounded them—the persistent drone of passing cars and scooters, the errant bark of a neighbor's dog—seemed to succumb to the music. By proximity and association, we were invited to the trio's semi-private revelry, bound by an unspoken agreement that our schedule for each new day could be placed on the back burner for a few moments.

When we climbed into our respective cars at week's end, my Finnish coworker observed that cultural bridges would always be of service wherever we found ourselves. Music, we concurred, was perpetually at (or at the very least near) the top of the list.

> *Music is the social act of communication among people, a gesture of friendship, the strongest there is.*
>
> —Malcolm Arnold

HAUNTING MEMORIES FROM THAILAND

Throughout this winter, I have spent an appreciable amount of time reflecting on past traveling adventures and perusing notes and letters written over that span of time.

Shuffling through my writings, I realized there was a strong correlation between how much I wrote about a particular country and how much I enjoyed my traveling experience in that country. Although I spent the same amount of time (two weeks) in Kuwait as I did in Bahrain, I wrote more than twice as much about my time in the latter—ditto for Indonesia and Malaysia.

Decidedly underrepresented was a two-week visit to Thailand in 2004. At the time, I fired off a couple of very brief e-mails to a few friends back home, touching on some of the high points (the Grand Palace, the Chatuchak weekend market, the breathtaking beaches, the reclining Buddha at Wat Pho). I also detailed the nightmare that is/was Bangkok traffic (unquestionably the worst traffic I have experienced anywhere in this wide world).

However, what leaps to mind when I reflect on my visit to Thailand has nothing to do with those memories. Bangkok and (nearby) Pattaya conjure up unspeakably horrific images for me.

I did not take a single photo in the red-light districts of Bangkok or Pattaya. One reason was that I knew the disturbing images would be seared into my memory for the remainder of my life. The other reason was sympathy and respect for the victims.

Children. Faces of children. Smiling at the passersby from behind plate-glass windows. Smiling with the lips, certainly not with the eyes: the "yim sao" smile (the smile of sadness). Panit, my driver for that week, explained to me that the reason the available women and children wore a variety of colored "labels" (blue, red, yellow, green, white) was to serve as a basic price guide. In general terms, the younger the trafficked sex worker, the higher the price.

Panit provided me with a brief summary of how the Thai sex trade worked. Was organized crime involved? Yes. Were the police involved? An almost imperceptible nod of the head. "Bottom line? It is good for the economy," he said. The majority of young girls and boys were and are trafficked from Burma, Cambodia, and other neighboring countries. Destitute parents sold some children, some were kidnapped, some were promised jobs, and some were simply collateral for debts gone bad.

I remember lying awake in my hotel bed at night feeling angry and utterly helpless. I was overwhelmed by a strident urge to grab one or two of these children and attempt to sneak them on the plane with me. As the saying goes, "Would it make a difference? For one or two children, it would."

> *Defeating human trafficking is a great moral calling of our time.*
>
> —Condoleezza Rice (PK)

SOUTH AFRICA / ZIMBABWE

Throughout the past week, I have explored hundreds of miles of African countryside and have also stopped for food and lodging in a few small towns. Curious looks were given (and received) as Cyril (my French coworker) and I smiled and greeted an array of men, women, and children.

Earlier in the week, we enjoyed watching multitudes of Zimbabwean school children walking (some barefoot, most with dusty shoes) to and from their little one-room schoolhouses. Most of the kiddos were friendly; more than a few went out of their way to deliver winning smiles (the younger ones anyway). The older children seemed to do a great job of looking after the little ones in their midst. While making our way around southern Africa, Cyril and I have been pleasantly surprised by the number of schools, even in the poorer townships.

Locals have quickly pointed out historic sites or interesting plants and animals. I remain awestruck by my encounters with immense baobab trees, some with trunks 30 to 40 feet in diameter—not circumference, diameter! On Wednesday we stopped for a particularly memorable picnic lunch under an immense baobab. While munching on a turkey sandwich, I found myself suspended in a three-dimensional daydream, designing a multi-level treehouse.

Late that afternoon, we crossed the Limpopo River and returned to the country of South Africa. As we approached our place of lodging for the night, we stopped for a red light at a busy intersection where I noticed a middle-aged woman asking for food. Regrettably, I had done a thorough job of devouring every scrap of food we had in the car (that should surprise no one), so I reached out to place a few South African rands in her hand. Memories of her face have faded, but I remember the touch of my hand to hers. Unquestionably, hers was the hardest palm I had ever come in contact with. It brought to mind the leather of my dad's wingtip shoes. I know I will lie in bed thinking and wondering about the life she has led.

South Africa (roughly equal in size to Texas and California combined) boasts an everchanging assortment of landscapes—mountains one day and then banana, sunflower, and sugar cane vistas the next. We have found vineyard after vineyard one day followed by parched desert. Cyril and I have seen only a handful of wild animals so far, but we are scheduled to meet up with a horde of coworkers this weekend at Kruger National Park. (Paying a visit to Kruger is the longest-standing item on my bucket list.)

Periodically, we have seen herds of wandering livestock. The chatty attendant who pumped our gas this afternoon asked if we had cows in America. Another man was surprised to learn that there were prostitutes in America. Interestingly, a couple of forthcoming locals have related that they associate the Afrikaans language (not English) with apartheid. "Afrikaans is the voice of much of our colonial past; English is the language of the Republic's future." Most southern Africans are multi-lingual; the Republic of South Africa has eleven official languages. Zimbabwe? Sixteen. Forty-three languages are spoken in Mozambique, including twenty-two with Bantu origins.

Throughout the weeks, a thought process has been running in my mind—sometimes in the background, sometimes in the forefront--the contrast between my own lifestyle and the lifestyle of the people around me. A couple of times this week, an ethereal voice from the radio (belonging to the siren, Dido) brought this thought process from the dim background to front and center. In her newly released song "Life for Rent" Dido reflects on commitment, perspective, authenticity, and connection. All pertinent topics for me in the context of my travels.

> *It is in your hands to make a better world for all who live in it.*
>
> —Nelson Mandela

SILVER THIEVES

Three coworkers and I spent the holiday (Chinese New Year) exploring Penang National Park. Penang is Malaysia's smallest national park but compensates with a showy display of breathtaking natural features—mountains, beaches, waterfalls, rainforest canopy walks, and freshwater swimming holes.

After climbing up, in, and around one of the larger canopy walks, we followed a trail to a swimming hole at the base of an engaging waterfall. We stopped at the water's edge to take in a peculiar site: self-advertised "monkey-proof" lockers. A few friendly locals who were drying off by a park bench strongly suggested that we take advantage of the lockers or risk losing everything to the ubiquitous, curious, silver-leaf monkeys. All four of us acted on the suggestion under a cacophony of chattering disdain from nearby tree limbs. After lunch, we would find similar lockers dotting the park's beaches.

While walking along the seashore, we encountered a distraught French couple who had ignored the warnings, only to find themselves up the proverbial creek without hats, sunglasses, or car keys. A park official assured them that the local rental car companies had extra sets of keys available for this very reason. I walked away wondering what percentage the monkeys received for the returned car keys. Wait a second. I am thinking small. The returned *cars*!

> *George promised to be good. But it is easy for little monkeys to forget.*
>
> —H.A. Rey

HONG KONG REVISITED

I knew, of course, before returning to Hong Kong that millions of people would be here. Also, I knew from experience that the American concept of "personal space" would not be cross-cultural. Okay. Got it. Prepared. *Wrong!* In my previous trip to the area, more than half of our work had taken place in the outlying areas, away from the city's center. Over the first few days of our current schedule, we updated the busiest streets Hong Kong has to offer.

I found myself flabbergasted by the amount of bodily contact that routinely takes place on the sidewalks of downtown Hong Kong. Please understand that I am not referring to brushing by. I mean, shoulder-to-shoulder collisions—NHL players "locked out" for the current season are flying here on a daily basis to join in the fray. One of my coworkers remarked, "It's not apathy; it's as if they want to run into you."

We walk Nathan Road each night in search of dinner, with the three men taking the lead, absorbing most of the direct hits on behalf of the three women who walk behind us. The personal space issue, though expected, is still hard to take. More than once I have been reminded of a friend's comment years ago at Disney World to a persistently pressing man standing in line behind her: "Excuse me, but could you get out of my ass?"

Town planners for Cary, North Carolina, must have recurring nightmares about Hong Kong. Suppose you own a business on Nathan Road or the surrounding area. The only parameters limiting the size and wattage of your sign are the amount of quarter-inch steel cable you can find and how much electricity you can afford. The nighttime glare makes Las Vegas look like a tired backwater. If visitors from another planet ever arrive in search of maintenance for their neon-illuminated vessels, I know exactly where their first stop should be.

For those of you who are fortunate enough not to dine with me on a regular basis, I am a "chickentarian." Give me a menu, and I will infallibly flip to the poultry section. Mention a chain restaurant, and I will recite my favorite chicken entrées. As I have traveled, I have found chicken dishes to be relatively safe and predictable. To date, I have ordered chicken dishes twice in Hong Kong and have twice been proffered substances that may qualify as avian on a molecular/DNA level but would surely be unrecognizable to Harland Sanders.

I am not sure exactly how chickens are processed here, but the end result is a pinkish, sinewy substance that more closely resembles processed jerky than any chicken I have ever encountered. On the other hand, maybe it is not the process but the birds themselves. What if, by some conflation of culture and ritualistic exercise, Hong Kong chickens spend their entire lives training for some sort of "Poultry Triathlon"? (Those ducks have such an advantage in the swimming leg of the competition.

Scary. Almost like they were born for the water.) A self-evident fact: More research is needed here.

Over the past couple of days, my driver and I have ventured far north of the City of Hong Kong, almost to the Chinese border (yes, there is still a border). People in the small villages there appear to be much less affected by Western culture. Many still wear traditional Chinese clothing. In addition, bilingual signs are few and far between, with the Queen's English all but disappearing. Judging from the stares I received, few Westerners visit these villages. I suppressed the urge to pull out my camera since my driver had informed me that the taking of photographs in those locales is viewed as both invasive and mocking. Today, my driver and I stopped at a small "restaurant" with a dirt floor and corrugated tin walls and roof. The kitchen/bathroom/butcher's block/laundry/foundry was in the back. For the second time on this trip, I opted for Plan B (a meticulous plan involving my backpack, bottled water, and some energy bars). I was tired, leery, and not up for a game of "Name That Vertebrate." My driver was very understanding.

I have watched enough Discovery Channel's *Animal Planet* shows to know that my sense of smell is not nearly as developed as my dog's. Nevertheless, I do find the smells of new places interesting and, in their own way, informative. Hong Kong has no shortage of smells; this is incontrovertible. Some are pleasant and some not-so-pleasant. Spices and other cooking-related smells—smells from the Pacific, traffic smells, and smells from the soil and vegetation—all swirl into a concoction of fragrances. Wherever I go, however, I invariably find that a fish will smell like a fish, and a garbage truck will smell like a garbage truck.

On the subject of constants, we have numbers. All around the world, hundreds of languages are spoken. Languages have evolved over countless centuries. Numbers? Base ten. That is a global constant. Even thousands of years ago, most folks had ten fingers—interesting thought. Simple, really, but it had never occurred to me until recently.

> *Hong Kong is a wonderful, mixed-up town where you've got great food and adventure. First and foremost, it's a great place to experience China in a relatively accessible way.*
>
> —Anthony Bourdain

SOUTH AFRICA, BOTSWANA

"The political history of South Africa is so fresh that those who lived through it are there to guide you. It's a rare chance to experience a country that is rebuilding itself after a profound change. The story of South Africa is a story of hope" (from my Lonely Planet Guide to South Africa).

Signs of the "profound change" in South Africa are on display everywhere in the cities and larger towns. Seeing how much change is possible in a relatively short time is encouraging. Figurative and literal doors that had been closed for fifty years are now standing open. On an ongoing basis, I am reminded that South Africans of all colors are rightly proud of their country, their new republic.

Earlier this month, we mapped a number of thoroughfares that interconnect the cities of Botswana. More recently, my coworker and I spent ten days driving narrow roads past and sometimes through several small villages in South Africa's Limpopo province.

One thing I remembered from my first trip and noticed again this month was people walking on the highways, sometimes barefoot on the hot asphalt. Every day, my coworker and I would wave to folks walking along, talking as they went, with not a hint of a house or building of any sort for miles in either direction. We pondered both the length of their walks and their reason(s). Once again, I was reminded of Robert Frost— "And miles to go before I sleep. And miles to go before I sleep." Mostly I thought of how little we Americans walk and the preparations and equipment we require when we do walk (cell phone, energy drink bottle, knee brace, sun hat, sunscreen, expensive exercise shoes, etc.).

On Monday we passed four children who had happened upon a prize by the side of the road. A sheet of corrugated tin, maybe 4 feet by 6 feet, had evidently been blown from a passing truck. The children had rescued the sheet from the grass and were, rather proudly, in the midst of taking it back to their village. The metal was too hot or too sharp to hold with their soft, young hands, so they had all taken off their shirts for use as "oven mitts" for the hot metal.

The following morning we passed an elementary school. The weather was pleasant, so we were driving with the windows down. A slight breeze delivered an olfactory echo from my own school days: mimeograph fluid. There's no mistaking that sharp smell, even from a distance. One whiff was all it took for me to be transported back to 1973 purple haze.

Soon after leaving the school, we happened upon a series of women with long machetes. Evidently, the provincial government was paying them to cut the long grass along the side of the road. Some of the women had their babies wrapped against their backs and were slinging their machetes full-tilt under the wilting African sun. That went on for miles—a relentless, elongated procession.

On Wednesday, Martin (my Swedish boss) and I stopped at a bed and breakfast near the city of Polokwane. Early the following morning, Martin took the wheel as we headed south on Highway 11. The next stop was Marblehall. As we verified road network attributes and admired the scenery, I remarked, "Look at the guy up ahead. He's driving on the wrong side of the road." Martin had, indeed, taken notice. The boneheaded driver remained in the same lane as his offending car drew closer. Our concern grew. After another tense moment, Martin and I jumped a bit in our seats following a worrisome, simultaneous revelation. "It's not him; it's us." Martin quickly steered the rental car to the left as the approaching Land Rover honked belligerently and blew past us.

Today is Sunday, and we enjoyed a welcomed day off. Our hotel lies in the midst of a large business district (Sandton) boasting tall, modern buildings with unexpected angles. Having grown tired of riding in cars, I decided to go for a morning walk. After meandering for a few blocks, I heard a loud voice and turned to identify the source. On the steps of a bank building, a man holding a well-worn Bible was leading an informal church service in the Xhosa language. The congregation was comprised solely of men, and I surmised that they had left their villages to come to the city to make money for the families they had left behind. Of course, I couldn't understand the man's words, but I sat on the margins, watched, and listened. I was able to figure out when prayer request time was and bowed for the prayers I felt but could not decipher. The unaccompanied hymns were beautiful, as was the simplicity of the service. This scene was as powerful as it was unexpected and hit me on an emotional and spiritual level that made my knees weak. I was sad to have missed the earlier part of the service, but I departed glad of heart, nonetheless.

> *South Africa gives me a perspective of what's real and what's not real.*
>
> —Dave Matthews

SOUTH STACK LIGHTHOUSE

On my way home from sunny South Africa, I once again met up with ASATC Anne. Together, we spent a couple days bicycling along the coast of Wales. Without question, one highlight was exploring a working lighthouse—South Stack Lighthouse—that had been constructed in 1809.

South Stack sits atop an islet that is fettered to the mainland by a bouncy, windblown, wooden bridge. To reach the lighthouse's lantern room, we climbed down 365 steep steps, crossed the bridge, and then scaled 118 winding steps inside the lighthouse. The wind was fierce, doubtless part and parcel with this location, but the sun warmed our faces.

The 360-degree view from the lantern room was spectacular, and the keeper was a genial host, ready to answer any and all questions. Long years after this visit, I find myself unable to conjure up the name of the keeper, but his border collie was named Griff.

Aside from chasing seagulls, Griff's sworn duty was post and package retrieval. In support of this endeavor, the keeper's wife had sewn a custom-made, blue canvas backpack for Griff, complete with Velcro fasteners. Whenever the postman or other delivery driver pulled into the lighthouse parking lot, Griff would sit (no doubt quivering with anticipation) just long enough for his boss to secure the backpack. Upon the keeper's command, Griff would launch himself down the 118 steps, across the bridge, and up the 365 steps of the mainland staircase—all in that piqued state of border collie hypervigilance—to accept delivery. "The Blue Blur," the keeper remarked as he described the process. If the delivery person arrived with more goods than the backpack could hold, Griff was more than happy to make multiple trips.

Anne and I tarried a bit in hopes that we would be granted an opportunity to see the Blue Blur in action but to no avail. Instead, we showered Griff with sweet talk and tummy rubs, apparently the standard treatment from lighthouse visitors. As we made our way to the bridge, I remarked, "I believe I just witnessed doggy nirvana."

> *Lighthouses don't go running all over an island looking for boats to save; they just stand there shining.*
>
> —Anne Lamott

MASIRAH ISLAND, OMAN

I am writing with a lot of time on my hands. Like Gilligan, I have found myself stranded on an island. Phones, lights, motorcars? Well, yes, we have those here, sort of. A working ferry to the mainland? That would be "no." Cyril and I had planned on spending one night on Masirah mapping the few quasi-paved roads on the island and poking our way around the "moonscape."

We were late (much too late) in discovering that the ancient diesel ferry that had deposited us on Masirah had given up the ghost upon its return to the mainland. This bit of unwelcome news had hardly arrived as a surprise. The 4-mile crossing to the lonely outpost had consisted of seventy-five minutes of an incessant, pulsating chugga-chugga-chugga from the boat's fatigued, faltering engine. I checked to see if Humphrey Bogart was at the helm.

Masirah Island is the largest island off the rocky coast of Oman. From north to south, the island is roughly 60 miles long. At its widest part, Masirah is a mere 8 miles across. During our tour of Masirah, Cyril and I stumbled upon an abandoned copper mine. These days, it appears that the lone industry is fishing. We stood on the island's shores and watched as timeless wooden dhows pulled nets around the shallow sea under the watchful eyes of seagulls. I have learned a bit about the history of the dhows of Oman. Over many centuries, generations of builders have never used any sort of blueprint. Each piece of wood is carefully cut to fit. As a result, no two dhows are identical.

Notable features of Masirah are wind, camels, fishing villages, and . . . 1970s vintage Land Rovers. The rusty, rumbling Rovers are the vehicle of choice, almost to exclusivity.

As our little misadventure played out, we arrived at the island's lone hotel. It was a no-frills establishment with perhaps twenty rooms. We made our appearance at the hotel desk around 5:30 p.m., only to find that the place was booked solid. The man at the desk was one of the very few islanders who spoke a smattering of English. He kindly directed us to a stable filled with animals—okay, not quite. The "annex" was a cement block building that fifty years prior had entertained deluded aspirations of earning a half-star. The annex was to civil engineering what *Caddyshack II* is to cinema. Asking no questions about rates, beds, amenities, or valet parking, we quickly grabbed the last two rooms in the annex. Having no idea when we might be able to return to the mainland, we booked two nights. As it turned out, we guessed correctly.

Our host motioned for us to sign in and then handed us our keys in exchange for our passports. (I always *hate* surrendering my passport, even in fancy, upscale hotels.) We lugged our suitcases and equipment up the cement staircase and found our rooms. Yes, the only available rooms were upstairs. That turned out to be a significant distinction since not a single room in the place was air-conditioned. Summertime. In the desert. Highs near 120 degrees, and nightly "lows" in the 90s. I briefly pondered swimming for the mainland. And that was before I stepped into my bathroom. The room was perhaps 5 feet by 4 feet with a sink on one wall and a spigot, garden hose, and threadbare towel on the opposite wall. Beneath the spigot, I found a 6-inch-by-6-inch hole in the floor. This corner would be my shower/toilet for the foreseeable future.

When I ventured next door to check on Cyril, I discovered that I had the better deal. Someone had appropriated his garden hose.

In order to get to sleep, we followed advice from a previous coworker who, in the 1950s, had spent time with the State Department in Saudi Arabia. Each night, we would take our top bed sheets, douse them in water, and then put the wet sheets over us. We were thus able to cool off enough to get some sleep. So thank you, Earl, wherever you are!

> *I had learned that in the same way that silence is a part of the conversation, patience is part of the rhythm of traveling.*
>
> —Rosita Boland

EASTERN CAPE (SOUTH AFRICA), LESOTHO

Klaus and I arrived in East London, South Africa, around sunset and checked into the Holiday Inn before grabbing a bite at a local diner. We had planned on spending four nights at this hotel but quickly changed our reservation to a single night after noticing that *all* the hotel's fire escape doors had been chained and padlocked. Not surprisingly, neither of us got much sleep that night.

In the morning, we took my driver Taki's suggestion and moved our belongings to a nearby B&B. It was a quaint little retreat run by a retired Swiss couple who seemed to embody every cheerful, wholesome quality one might expect from former school teachers. They welcomed us with tea and stories, and before we knew it, we'd settled in for the rest of our East London stay. Each evening, Klaus and I found ourselves chatting about local lore and history in their cozy sitting room. Our convivial hosts were delighted to share humorous stories from their teaching days, stories that left us laughing well into the night.

On our third day in East London, I chatted with Taki and related some of the stories I had heard at the B&B. Taki (around age 50) began to reminisce about his school days in the nearby town of Ginsberg. I was floored to learn that he had been a childhood neighbor of the anti-apartheid activist and martyr Stephen Biko. In turn, Taki was amazed to know that I had heard of Biko. In retrospect, I have been puzzled to find that few streets in South Africa have been named for Stephen Biko or Bishop Desmond Tutu. In comparison, nearly every town has a Nelson Mandela Street or Boulevard.

After our enjoyable time in East London, Klaus left to assist with the mapping of Cape Town as I bid farewell to our two drivers. I grabbed my suitcase and backpack, climbed into the rental car, and headed northward. It was time to meet up with an American coworker in the mountains of Lesotho. In a bustling restaurant in downtown Maseru (the country's capital and largest city), I found Stuart. Together, we successfully secured rooms in a hotel that featured operating fire escape doors.

Our visit was in January (mid-summer), so we did not encounter snow. However, the nights were cooler than we had anticipated, so we dressed in layers. While there, we learned that the *lowest* elevation in the entire country is an astonishing 4,600 feet above sea level. Lesotho is a small country, about the size of Massachusetts and Connecticut combined, and is completely surrounded by the Republic of South Africa.

We found the people of Lesotho to be welcoming—and curious. Almost every time we stopped, we ended up explaining the purpose of our wires, antennas, and computers. Some locals thought we were pulling their collective leg. Conversations were rather limited as English speakers were few in number (when compared to their South African counterparts), and my knowledge of the Sesotho language is, well, nonexistent.

Hotels were not common, and we often ended up in Colonial Era boarding houses. A couple of the rural establishments that we patronized did not offer access to television or refrigeration. On the plus side, we felt safe walking about at night and reveled in the exotic noises (mostly nocturnal birds, amphibians, and insects) as we walked.

As is the case in dozens of African nations, AIDS is an epidemic throughout Lesotho. Even in the smallest villages, we noticed busy undertakers and grave diggers struggling to keep pace with demands for their services. The pall of death was palpable. One of the lasting images from my time in Lesotho will be the crowded orphanages. Of that I am certain. The other lasting image will be of the surrounding mountaintops—beauty and heartbreak bounded by jagged horizons on all sides.

> *Listen, drink the sun's rays with joy, with light, and a peaceful heart. Listen, drink the sun's rays with love, with death, then the stars above.*
>
> —K. Sello Dulker

BBC

For the majority of my travels, the BBC was my steadfast companion, often the only English-speaking channel in a sea of incomprehensible television. (Now I'm remembering a Bill Bryson quip: "The best that can be said for Norwegian television is that it gives you the sensation of a coma without the worry and inconvenience.")

I was deeply grateful for the BBC's tireless dedication to the deliverance of breaking news events from around the world, no matter where my travels took me. Over the years, the BBC dutifully introduced major stories—Athens and the Summer Olympics, the heart-wrenching siege of child hostages in Chechnya, Al Qaeda attacks in Spain, the unimaginable devastation of the tsunami in Indonesia, and later the chaos of Hurricane Katrina.

One particular stay in Riyadh, Saudi Arabia, cemented my appreciation for the BBC's steadying presence. Seven coworkers and I had been assured that the Saudi government had formally greenlighted permission for our mapping project. Upon arrival, however, we learned that "greenlight" had been an optimistic interpretation; we were informed that we would be stuck in neutral for an indefinite period while "formalities" were ironed out (though "palms greased" felt infinitely closer to the mark). As a result, we spent nearly a week marooned in a state of lethargy, stuck in a bureaucratic fog without a single productive thing to occupy our time. Days passed in a blur of card games, room service, occasional visits to the bowling alley across the street, and the BBC. Fredrik, our Finnish coworker, took the lull especially hard. We were stranded in a desert, both literally and figuratively. The (ahem) absolute absence of vodka weighed heavily on him. "*Ollako vai eikö*" ("To be or not to be").

> *Radio and television are like corridors through which the whole of life passes. If we've witnessed the dramas of history—wars, natural disasters, sporting spectacles—it's generally been through the media. Yet the BBC has always done far more than reflect the contemporary. Since 1922 it's been one of the most influential forces shaping it.*
>
> —David Hendy

PART 5:
A NEW HOME BASE: SMALL TOWN WEST VIRGINIA

SWIM TIME

(I like to keep my friends back in North Carolina up to date on the goings on here in Small Town, West Virgina. The following is one "press release.")

I keep hearing how exercise will help my state of mind. *Not!*

Last night I decided to venture over to the local college pool for a quick swim. Upon arrival, I discovered that I would be sharing the lanes and locker room with the local boys' high school swim team. Like me, they were putting in their laps before closing time, albeit with about five times the vigor.

When the lights began to dim, signaling the pool's imminent closing, I made my way to the showers. As I stood in the midst of a crowd of lean, tireless teenage athletes, a familiar voice echoed in my head—the voice of Marlin Perkins from *Wild Kingdom*. Marlin narrated a scene from the African savannah. In his low, conspiratorial tone, he described a herd of impalas sipping at a watering hole, blissfully unaware that a pride of lions had already singled out the slowest, most feeble individual in their number. I picked up the pace.

Keenly familiar with my penchant for self-deprecation, I tried to tune out Marlin's voice as I dressed. Surely, I thought, the age gap wasn't so painfully obvious. Perhaps I wasn't, in fact, a plodding relic from a forgotten geologic era with all (well, most) of the grace of an arthritic tortoise. Quite possibly, these boys did not see me as a fossil with legs—or at the very least not entirely.

When the last member of Generation X-Box 360 left the locker room, he encountered his coach.

Coach: "Are you the last one?"

Teen: "Naw, coach, that, uh, that old guy is still in there." I thought of several inappropriate retorts:

"Hey, you try showering and dressing while dragging this oxygen tank around with you!"

"My private-duty nurse can kick your nanny's backside!"

"How long will it take you to ride home on that GI Joe Power Wheels Jeep of yours?"

(Sigh)

If you need me this morning, I will be here in my pajamas, eating oatmeal and watching *Matlock*.

> *Enjoy swimming for swimming's sake. We have to spend far too much time in the water to not enjoy the process of challenging yourself, of moving through the water.*
>
> —Jeff Rouse

ILL-ADVISED LUNCH DATE

I actually had a lunch date today—bizarre notion, I know. The meet-up had been arranged by a coworker in Pittsburgh who had (previously) been a trusted friend. My blind date and I met at a nice restaurant in Bridgeport, West Virginia. The food was plentiful and delicious. Under most circumstances, I would have enjoyed every morsel.

The topics of conversation were her hair, her job, her status in the community, and how (financially) successful she was compared to her siblings and school chums. Also, in painstaking detail, she described how she was still a size 4 and simply would not, could not "let myself go like so many women my age" (forty-two).

It took my date a good ten minutes to place her salad order: "I would like for the free-range cucumbers to be artfully arranged on top of the salad; fair-trade balsamic vinaigrette dressing on the side, shaken not stirred. Also, have them remove the stems from my mushrooms before slicing them. The croutons are not domestic, are they?" Okay, so I embellish a smidge.

When she left to go powder her dainty little nose, I will admit that I was secretly hoping she would, on returning to our table, waltz through the crowded restaurant with the hem of her size 4 skirt wedged in the waistline of her size 4 pantyhose so her size 4 posterior would become the butt of many a joke. I know. I am bad.

The meal was a tedious, seventy-five-minute endeavor.

The following day, I learned that my date was a member of a genetic subspecies: "Very High Maintenance Woman" (VHMW). The VHMW is a carbon-based life form. However, due to generations of über selective and exceedingly limited mating rituals, the subspecies has been left with only vestigial traces of the warmth typically associated with mammals.

I filed the previous evening away under the heading of "Lesson Learned."

I've been on so many blind dates, I should get a free dog.
—Wendy Liebman

FAREWELL, GARDEN CITY BEACH

I am a Methodist PK. I grew up wandering from parsonage to parsonage in western North Carolina. A weighty awareness that I would soon be moving to a new town and a new school dwelled perpetually in my subconscious. Like a "military brat," I was destined for a childhood of impermanence involving a succession of disorienting, destabilizing relocations. Throughout my formative years, three places overflowed with warm and reassuring experiences and thus became my adopted homes: Garden City Beach, South Carolina; my grandparents' home in Matthews, North Carolina; and Lake Junaluska, North Carolina.

Garden City Beach has always displayed a talent for reinventing itself: enduring hurricanes, relentless tides of real estate fever, and a self-harming commercial ambition. But before I returned there last week, I'd underestimated just how much change had seeped into every corner. My first clue was an abandoned building along US 17: a Krispy Kreme that once proudly signaled the turn toward the beach. Upon my unannounced return, the red and green trim barely clung to the old brick; the building looked embarrassed, standing there forlorn and empty. I tried to avert my gaze out of respect, only to be greeted by a neon sign that proudly announced, "The Pink Pony Gentlemen's Club."

In earlier years, I had gently slipped back into Garden City, though too often only to discover that one more piece of my childhood had quietly vanished—the old soda fountain, the miniature golf course, Everett's Yum-Yum Shoppe, and the Bamboo Motel (for decades the only lodging option for those with no family cottage). The motel had been there from my earliest beach memories with its neon sign humming through the night. I wandered over to the Garden City Arcade, the place that had once devoured my dimes with endless games of skeeball and baseball. The arcade was still there, but flashy, reverberating electronic gizmos had replaced the classic games. It stung like a sore tooth.

Hurricane Hugo had swept away the old cottages long ago—my grandfather's, my great-uncle's, and those of their friends who had made their own late-in-life pilgrimages from towns to the north and west. These days, the beachfront is stacked with multi-storied condos so Garden City's profile blends into every other glitzy mile of the Grand Strand. As for the people who made Garden City feel like home, most of them left long before Hugo barreled through, gone to a higher shore where time and tide don't wear down the landscape.

In my occasional visits over the last twenty years, I have determinedly clung to scraps of memory, hoping to retain a glimmer of the past—a child licking an orange push-up would suffice. But time has a way of stealing things in broad daylight.

Hugo may have torn down cottages, but the years took away more. They took the people and places that had once offered a cherished reassurance.

Arriving there last week, I felt a bit like the character of Willy Loman—Arthur Miller describes him as "a little ship in search of a harbor." But what remained was the whisper of memories fading like old songs (cue "Beach Baby" by The First Class). I lingered, feeling the emptiness as if standing on the edge of something washed away forever.

Garden City Beach, South Carolina, is no more. Can't get there from here. "My" Garden City has been swept away by the scouring dimension of time. I can no more drive to Garden City than I can walk into my grandparents' kitchen to find my grandfather standing over the stove in his faded apron, flipping pancakes and turning to smile at me.

Nothing is ever really lost to us as long as we remember it.
—L.M. Montgomery

A LAUGH AT LAGUARDIA

Last night I was making travel plans for an upcoming training event. As it turned out, my itinerary would take me through New York's LaGuardia Airport. The mere mention of LaGuardia brings to mind a singular memory from several years ago.

On a rainy afternoon I sat in LaGuardia's expansive baggage claim area waiting patiently to see my much-abused suitcase tumble out of the chute and flop onto the baggage carousel like an inebriated walrus. I waited from a safe distance. This was hardly my first foray to New York, so I recognized the futility of battling aggressive locals as they jostled for position at the luggage chute. Doubtless, I would fare better showing my dead gazelle claim check to a pride of lions.

As I waited, my attention was drawn to a young family seated nearby. To be more precise, only the parents and their three-year-old son were sitting. The six-year-old daughter was skillfully "driving" a four-wheeled luggage cart through the crowd, a look of dogged determination on her cherubic face. She was gripping the handlebar like a steering wheel, intermittently "honking" the pretend horn in the center of the bar. As she deftly made a quick left turn by a support column, she commandingly shouted, "Out of the way, ****-for-brains!"

I stifled a laugh and glanced over at the parents. The mother was glaring daggers at the father who, in turn, was looking for the nearest bunker.

> *Children are the future, but they often don't get enough credit for how bright they are. They're always listening and observing, and their little brains are soaking up information like sponges. But another thing about kids is that they're basically tiny little comedians.*
>
> —Adelaide May Ross

IT ALL BEGAN WITH AN INNOCENT-LOOKING PACKAGE UNDER THE CHRISTMAS TREE

As I was opening one of my Christmas presents from Amy, she produced her registered nurse card and deftly played it.

The present was a new pillow. By some stretch of healthcare logic, she had reached the conclusion that my old pillow was, in essence, a miniature Superfund site. Amy paused to ask how long I had been using the relic. I had to stop and think. Remember when the US hockey team beat the Soviets in Lake Placid? Yeah. 1980. Perhaps Amy had a point.

In a somber ceremony, I removed my old pillow from the bed and, with much ceremony, replaced it. We boxed the old pillow up and mailed it to the CDC in Atlanta.

The problem with my new pillow was that it was too fat. Over the years, my head and neck had become accustomed to a flattened pillow. Pillow surgery would be needed. I opened one of the pillow's seams about an inch and a half and was, in a matter of seconds, fairly covered in what marketers at the pillow factory call microbeads. The tiny white beads flew everywhere. In no time, our living room looked like the morning after an all-nighter at John Belushi's house. After allowing a third of the beads to float out of the pillow, I stitched up the seam as best I could.

I attempted the microbead cleanup when Amy was out running errands. Plan A involved a broom and a dustpan. The inherent problem was that the beads steadfastly refused to be swept. The broom only angered and dispersed the beads. Plan B involved Amy's Dyson vacuum cleaner—a beast that I had unsuccessfully battled in previous months. This particular Dyson has more attachments and parts than my twenty-year-old Volvo (and weighs almost as much). Doubtless, it has a higher resale value and better acceleration.

I had watched Amy use the vacuum on many occasions and had tried my best to learn how to operate it. With a series of swift, deft movements, she can clean a floor, a curtain, a light fixture, or a kitchen cabinet. With a couple of additional twists, she can grant wishes for godchildren, conduct the Pittsburgh Symphony Orchestra, and fend off Darth Vader.

Having no other cleaning implements at my disposal, I cautiously removed the dreaded yellow Dyson Beast from its confines in the basement. My choices were very limited: put my own health and well-being at risk by plugging the thing in or explain to Amy that (after eighteen years of schoolin') I was incapable of cleaning a living room floor.

The first option was slightly more palatable, so I released the Beast. I rolled the contraption across the floor where it proceeded to suck up . . . nothing. With pensive hand to chin, I noticed that the only part of the machine with any suction was the top of the handle. Over the course of many months, I had time and again watched Amy remove a long cylinder from said handle for use as a wand/baton/suck-saber. Alas, try as I might, I could not figure out how to remove Excalibur from the stone.

Exasperated, I found the Beast's center of gravity and hoisted the thing off the ground. I leaned the (loudly sucking) handle forward and straddled the vacuum—my feet and legs akimbo—as I hunched over. With my customary grace, I proceeded to pivot the thing to and fro in an oscillating motion, one slow, lunging step after another. The beads slowly disappeared. I felt very much like a parent holding a toddler as it learned to swim in a foot of water. The difference? I completed the task with no hug, no dignity, no gleam of pride, and certainly no sense of accomplishment.

Well, if nothing else, I was able to provide entertainment for the dogs.

> *And I saw a beast coming out of the basement. It had ten horns and seven heads, with ten crowns on its horns, and on each head a blasphemous name.*
> —Revelation 13:1 (Household Appliance Version)

BIC RAZOR BLUES

Once again I find myself on the road, encumbered with the usual nonessentials (plenty of non-Michelle-Obama-approved junk food, USB drives filled with an incongruous and eclectic mix of songs, my scavenger-hunt list, and enough books to serve as ballast).

If you find yourself wondering if I had forgotten at least one essential, you have, quite sagely, never ventured out on the highways with me.

This time, the overlooked necessity was my razor. I knew I could stop by a drugstore and purchase a new razor and four or five blades for roughly the cost of installing a Central American banana republic.

Being my father's son, I purchased the cheapest package of disposable razors that Walgreens had on their shelves. I even used my registered phone number to get the Walgreens discount. The package read "BIC Comfort 3," hereafter referred to as "BIC Misnomer 3."

When I had finished scraping 40 percent of the whiskers off my face, I noticed that 38 percent of my facial skin was in the sink. At that same moment, I noticed a disheveled, wide-eyed, pink glob of cotton candy mocking me from the bathroom mirror. He had even borrowed my favorite "Life is Good" T-shirt. The cruelest irony. If I had attempted to apply aftershave, the coroner's photo would be Exhibit A for the local college's workshop on spontaneous combustion.

If I had been locked in my own garage, I could have achieved the same result (and saved $6.99) with my mower blade or a sheet of 200-grit sandpaper.

When I return to work next week, I am sure the regulars there will be eager to learn what exfoliating tragedy has befallen me. My ready answer: I climbed Mount Everest.

> *The best reason I can think of for not running for President of the United States is that you have to shave twice a day.*
>
> —Adlai Stevenson

SEVEN YEARS IN TIBET (CONDENSED TO ONE AFTERNOON)

Last night I went for a walk in the woods behind the local high school—quiet time interrupted only by an Eastern phoebe, a rufous-sided towhee, and one raucous blue jay. I did not see a single woodland mammal, but I did manage to find myself—always a good and necessary thing.

On the way back to my old Volvo, I passed the high school's oval track. In the fading light, the track looked outsized to the point of intimidation. My mind "raced" back to days of running on the (not-always-level) track behind my old high school. I sat for a moment and gazed at the present-day track, remembering the days of yore when I could cover the distance of the oval in well under a minute or sprint halfway around the track to hand the baton to the relay anchor, my buddy John.

Sigh. Once upon a time I could run fast. I could take one step and dunk a basketball. These days, it hurts when I rise from my chair. As I wistfully longed for the days of my youth and the accompanying abilities, a thought hit me: One day (twenty years from now?) I could very well be looking out a window, wistfully wishing I could go for a walk in the woods. The perspective that intertwined with the thought hit me—hard.

I hope I can adjust a bit more gracefully as I continue to age and that I find appreciation in what I can do today without getting tripped up by my yesterdays.

Whatever age you are is the right age.

—Morrie Schwartz

PART 6:
SENIOR DOGS, SENIOR MOMENTS, AND THE ADVENT OF "POPPY"

MY LAZY GIRL

My chair is a La-Zy-Boy recliner. It is for reading, watching television, working sudoku puzzles, and napping. In most circumstances, the footrest is in use.

When a TV show, book, puzzle, or nap has ended, the footrest is lowered with a clunky pa-THUNT sound—an ending, for the chair. The pa-THUNT sound for eons heralded a beginning for my faithful border collie, Sallie. She would unwaveringly be found within arm's length, resting and waiting for the echoing pa-THUNT. At this audible signal, she would leap to her feet (until her later years near the end of her life when she would rise cautiously, struggling gamely).

For Sallie, pa-THUNT was a call to action. It was Holmes emphatically remarking to Watson, "The game is afoot!" It was the red light on the Bat Phone. It was Paul Revere. Sallie would make eye contact to let me know she was ready for the new challenge or adventure. "Do you need help retrieving the laundry from the basement?" "Are there unauthorized mammals in the yard?" "Is it time to patrol the block?" "Do we need to put that book away and choose another one?" "Do we have an overabundance of pepperoni rolls in the kitchen?" The reason for my getting up mattered not to Sallie. She was ever at the ready. Sallie regarded all my activities with eager fascination. My movements were not to be missed, and she would intrepidly accompany me, come hell or high water.

These days, I still spend considerable amounts of time in my recliner. Without thinking, I lower the footrest, hear pa-THUNT, and subconsciously expect (yearn) to hear those paws scratch for traction on the hardwood floor. Nothing. The silence is all- encompassing. The emptiness finds me.

I have no doubt that my Sallie is undertaking a new series of adventures these days, but here in my chair, I realize yet again that it is always harder for the one left behind.

> *If you've ever seen a dog age, you'll know: Their death comes too slowly and entirely too fast, all at once.*
>
> —Shay Castle

A TRIO OF CASE STUDIES

Back in the summer, I attended a conference in Greater Metropolitan Flatwoods, West Virginia. At breakfast on Day 1, I sauntered down to the hotel's restaurant to make an appreciable dent in the breakfast buffet. On the way to my Naugahyde booth, I couldn't help but notice as a woman in her mid-forties placed her own breakfast plate heavily on her table. The contents: seven sausage patties. Mesmerized, I watched in disbelief (disgust) as she began spreading butter on top of the patties. I lost my breakfast appetite: the rarest of occurrences.

Fast forward a couple of years. As Amy and I were driving to Weston one afternoon, I noticed a guy heading in the opposite direction. The man sat astride a rolling mid-life crisis. I would later learn that this contraption was a Can-Am "Slingshot," a $30,000 tricycle. My comment to Amy: "It never ceases to amaze, the crazy things people do with their money."

And then, last week I was taking Sassy (Sallie's successor) on her early morning walk. From half a block away, we watched a mom and her fifth-grade daughter climb into a car. As we continued our walk, the mom drove 230 feet to her daughter's school, dropped her offspring off at the school's front door, and then circled the block to return to her driveway. Our attempts at looking the other way were . . . ineffectual. Sassy and I took turns asking each other for some manner of explanation for this behavior on a clear, 65-degree morning.

What do these three events have in common? For all three of these brief encounters, I was perched upon my high horse.

First, if charged with maintaining an unhealthy diet, I would have to throw myself on the mercy of the court. I periodically have nightmares where I find myself being pursued by kale and spinach. The "trike"? Pulling out my own checkbook for a self-audit never fails to be humbling. And here's the thing: I am not an impulse buyer. That means I continue to sit down, deliberate, rationalize, and *then* spend money on purchases that, in retrospect, comprise a laughable litany open to ridicule. As for choosing driving over walking, once again I must self-incriminate.

I have a print-out of a simple continuum at my desk, just above my monitor. Its purpose? To remind me that I am no better and no worse than my neighbors; I'm simply (on any given day) at a different spot on a continuum.

> *We are all fools in some way, and most of us in more ways than we know.*
>
> —*François de La Rochefoucauld*

PRIUS ENCOUNTER

Care to be entertained? Put a fifty-eight-year-old "late adopter" in the driver's seat of a rented Prius . . . with no owner's manual (yours truly last week).

After a few initial humorous fumblings, I did manage to (1) start the car and (2) use the little joystick thingy (industry term) to put the car in drive. Curiously, the little Nintendo screen gave four options: R, N, D, and B. I remain blissfully unenlightened as to what the B's purpose might be. Bounce? Blast off? Bifurcate?

Driving the Prius was not significantly different from driving a conventional car. The Crisis de Prius occurred after I had reassured myself that I was a competent hybrid operator. Ah, but parking would prove to be my unexpected nemesis. After arriving at my first destination, the time came to shift the Prius into park. Hmmmm. R, N, D, and the perplexing B. For all the ice cream in the world, I could not perform this basic task. I tried all the gear positions twice and then decided that a bit more leverage would solve my dilemma. After dislocating my shoulder, turning the air scarlet with my vocabulary, and leaving incisor/cuspid marks on the steering wheel, I turned to

Amy. "What is that button over there with the P?" she asked. Me: "I don't know. I think it is the parking brake." With curious caution, I pushed it. Nothing. Nada.

Next, I opened the driver's door to look for a "West Virginia" solution (e.g., throw a stick of firewood behind each wheel). A disembodied voice responded, "This is highly irregular, Dave." Intimidated, I closed the door. My next thought involved forcibly removing the aforementioned joystick from its cradle in the dashboard.

Meanwhile, Amy went off to play nurse to a frightened young mother who had been watching me with one hand deep in her purse, no doubt gripping her canister of mace.

Once again, I worked my way through the gear selections, this time with my left foot feverishly pounding the floorboard, searching in vain for the nonexistent clutch. I began grinding my teeth, only stopping when a blood vessel in my left eye burst. I glanced at the rearview mirror and was alarmed to find Chief Inspector Dreyfus from the Pink Panther movies casting a deranged look in my direction.

"This can't be this hard!" I told myself. "Brian Griffin drives a Prius, and he doesn't even have opposable thumbs!"

The 143rd thing I tried was pushing the P button with the gear selector in the N mode, my foot on the brake, and the rear window defogger on. Voila! I had managed to put the Prius in park. A wave of relief hit me. I remember thinking to myself, "A room full of monkeys with typewriters."

> *Japanese engineers who enjoy playing practical jokes are overdue for an avalanche of karma.*
>
> —Allen Cook

SASS FACTOR

Some twenty months ago, Sassy and I agreed to adopt each other. Although we were both a bit long in the tooth, we mutually decided that we were up for the challenges and rewards of growing older with each other.

Sassy has proved to be an understated, understanding, compassionate, and even-tempered member of the family. She was a calming presence in the midst of COVID-19. As far as my home office, Sassy is eager to contribute her efforts and suggestions and serve as my canine confidante.

On our morning and evening walks, she never tires of my interminable ramblings, nonsensical non-sequiturs, wince-inducing plays on words, whiney complaints, and off-key attempts at singing. She is on the receiving end of knowing looks from neighborhood pooches. Her cross to bear. Bless her heart.

My conversations with Sassy run the gamut of topics. Frequently, I seek her opinions and blunderingly attempt to pry into her guarded past—Sassy's first ten years with her previous owner. I want to hear her backstory. Her expressive brown eyes tell me, "I've had happy and sad days. I have wonderful memories, not unlike the ones you share with me." And then, "I'd much rather be present. I have you. You have me. We have today. Let that be our focus, please." That's followed matter-of-factly with "I would not be opposed to another stroll around the neighborhood."

> *We don't quite treat them [dogs] like were talking to each other, or to babies, but we often let them in our most private thoughts. We converse with them. Their role is singular.*
>
> —Alexandra Horowitz

. . . IN WHICH POPPY RECEIVES A FAILING GRADE

A certain three-and-a-half-year-old comes for visits on a regular basis. That pleases me immeasurably. One of William's favorite activities is "driving" Poppy's car or, preferably, Mamie's car. We spend quality time in the garage as William buckles himself in the driver's seat. Off we go—to the store, to his aunt's house, to work, back home, back to the store. With a practiced hand, he "drives" around town, stopping periodically for stop signs, fire trucks, little old ladies, or wandering dogs.

He let me "drive" Mamie's car for a while today. I was heading down the road, destination grocery store, when he asked me to roll his window down. My incredulous reply was that, quite unfortunately, I could not roll his window down as the car key was back inside the house. William leveled me with The Look as I began to explain why we needed a key to open Mamie's windows but that no key was needed to roll down the windows in Poppy's old car. The look was a mix of pity and worn patience. He took a deep breath and carefully explained, with a measured tone reserved for the irretrievably dense, that he had been referencing the pretend window.

Sigh. Remedial Poppy School is required. Not sure how we will scrape up the tuition, but if William is involved, I am convinced that Her Mamie-ship will find a way.

> *Humankind cannot bear very much reality.*
>
> —T. S. Eliot

SNOW DAYS

Over the past three days, Sassy and I have enjoyed snowy neighborhood walks. The pleasing sights and echoing sounds transcend time. Two predominant and contrasting sounds meet our ears: maniacal, excited shrieks from neighborhood kids and harsh scraping noises (along with associated mumbled grumblings) from car windshields and parents—two sides of a frozen coin.

Sassy (now eleven years old) and I (fast approaching sixty) watch from the hilly margins as sled after sled of boisterous, cherry-cheeked children speed by, followed closely (and encouraged frantically) by their respective dogs--markedly younger versions of ourselves.

After vicariously reveling in these activities, Sassy and I return to our walk, each thankful for opportunities to take in the ongoing wintry spectacle.

Rosebud!

—Charles Foster Kane

SPICING THINGS UP

Monday morning, Sydney, Australia: Don't know if you caught this bit on the news, but a woman encountered a 10-foot-long python in the spice aisle of her grocery store. Think about that.

Sydney is the largest city in the country. Five million people. Grocery store. In short, is there anywhere in this sizable country where you should *not* be worried about the presence of snakes?

Quite fortunately, the young woman who found the 10-footer staring at her (from inches away) was a trained snake catcher. Wondering here: An Aussie who is trained to catch snakes, is that comparable to an American who has been trained to . . . use a remote?

At any rate, the young woman, who looks to weigh all of 110 pounds, alerted the store's staff upon spying the python. Subsequently, she dashed home and retrieved her snake bag (again, Australia). Sans assistance, she guided the python into her bag and then drove to a nearby wood to release the beast.

So many things about this news item confound me. The largest city I have called home is Atlanta. After reading this story,

I began to imagine a similar event at Kroger in Emory Village. My mind, predictably, activated its own YouTube channel, complete with looping videos: a SWAT team; Tom Cruise rappelling from a helicopter; scores of scampering, screaming patrons; ambulances; a cadre of lawyers; multiple calls to the governor; napalm; the Emory Village Fire Department's response to pleas of "Get here fast and burn this $%#^&@%# building to the ground"; cardiac fatalities; a caped Andre the Giant standing in a wheelbarrow in the middle of Aisle 4 intoning "There will be no survivors!"

The soundtrack accompanying the spliced videos of wild-eyed desperation and panic? Led Zeppelin's "Immigrant Song."

There was no imaginable scenario in which the snake lived to be released in the nearby woods. Fatalities would be involved for at least two species.

Just to be on the safe side, I will now be avoiding the spice aisle at my grocery store. As my cautious neighbor would say, "Can't never tell."

> *But don't worry. Most snakes don't want to hurt you. If you're out in the bush and a snake comes along, just stop in your tracks and let it slide over your shoes.*
>
> —Australian tour guide offering serpentine advice to a resolutely incredulous Bill Bryson

ELEVATOR INTERLUDE

This morning I made a new friend in the hotel elevator. The cutest four-year-old boy in all of Scranton, Pennsylvania, attempted to leave the elevator on Level 2, mistakenly concluding that since the doors had opened, the car must have reached the lobby level. Watchful Dad and amused me both offered our hands to guide the winsome spark plug back to the starting blocks.

As the elevator doors closed, I regarded the boy. Being conversant in four-year-old, I complimented the boy's Paw Patrol light-up shoes. "Who is your favorite Paw Patrol Pup?" He gave me an assessing look and replied, "Rubble!" "He does likes to dig!" commented the father. Additional information was forthcoming. "I also like Mayor Goodway 'cause she looks like my grandma." "Ah," I replied. "That Chickaletta is forever getting into trouble." My new friend concurred. The affable dad smiled.

My next (predictable) line: "I really like your dinosaur." The boy tilted his head to gaze at the stuffed animal perched in his little hands and responded, "He is a good dinosaur. His name is

George." Me: "It is a relief to hear that he is a good dinosaur. I would hate to be eaten this early in the morning. Why did you name him George?" The boy looked up, surmised that I was more than a bit slow on uptake, and responded: "I didn't name him. George is just who he is."

The three actors in this impromptu production stepped off the elevator at the lobby level, issuing courteous wishes for an adventurous new day.

Here's the thing. I missed my first elevator car this morning because I had to return to my hotel room to fetch my COVID mask. Otherwise, I would have missed this heart-warming kick-off to the new day. Call it a Happy Accident if you like; I prefer serendipity . . . or providence.

> *Any work that is born out of natural serendipity, or reverts to simpler times, is poignant for people—in any era.*
>
> —Cai Guo Qiang

SIBLING SOLIDARITY

I spent last week at the beach. My assigned duty involved playing goalie for the two grandkids: stop them and kick them back into play when called upon.

In this capacity, I had plenty of time to people-watch. Amongst the frenetic swarm of vacationers surrounding me, I paid particular notice to a pair of teenage sisters. I'm guessing they were sixteen and seventeen years of age.

My initial assessment of the pair brought to mind the noted sociologist John Bender. To paraphrase, "School would probably shut down if they didn't show up. The queenies aren't here!"

The sisters featured impossibly long legs; flawless skin; 500-watt smiles; high cheekbones; stylish bikinis; and full, glistening, bouncing, shoulder-length brown hair. Both sisters effused a Hepburn-esque level of measured self-assuredness.

As I watched them, I pieced together their likely schedules back at their home: co-captains of volleyball and tennis teams, equestrian events, cello recitals, French club, and student government meetings. I found myself wondering if their principal and guidance counselor ran their ideas by these sisters before implementing them.

As surely as night follows day, an endless procession of doors will be held open for these girls in the years and decades ahead.

Now, the Rest of the Story. The most noticeable, remarkable, and memorable thing about these sisters was their relationship with their younger brother Gary (age thirteen?). Though markedly shorter than his two big sisters, Gary featured that same winning smile and a head of bouncing brown hair. Other similarities were few. You see, Gary was born with Down syndrome.

Everywhere the sisters went (walking on the beach, floating in the lazy river, playing shuffleboard, sipping Cokes under their umbrella, making new friends), they made sure that Gary was in a tight orbit. The trio was demonstrably inseparable. The parents, like me, were sitting in the margins watching, taking it all in. Doubtlessly proud beyond proud of their three children.

> *A story is something that happens that you didn't expect, that leads to some internal change in yourself: a change that helps you feel more connected to life, makes it more spacious and welcoming.*
>
> —Anne Lamott

NEW EYES

Throughout my sixty-one years on this earth, I have from time to time pondered insightful words of wisdom attributed to the Greek philosopher Heraclitus: "No man ever steps in the same river twice, for it's not the same river and he's not the same man." Until the past year and for reasons unknown, I had focused on changes in the river, failing to consider the concurrent changes in me.

For fourteen of the last fifteen years, I have resided in Buckhannon, West Virginia, with a population of 5,400 (Salute!). My county (Upshur) is home to only 23,000 people, but it is (in square miles) larger than the country of Singapore. Upshur is also home to eight stoplights.

Completely unaccustomed to remaining in one town for so long, I am vulnerable to slipping into an unappreciative state of monotony. Sedentary spells nibble away at my curiosity and, if left unchecked, may cast a dull pall over my days. As a partial remedy, I watch movies and TV shows set in far-flung locales. I yearn to explore those exotic places in person, to lose myself in the grand theater of the unfamiliar.

To my knowledge, my Sassy (age twelve or thirteen) has never read philosophy. Nonetheless, she is my tireless mentor. As the rising sun greets each new day, Sassy charges out our front door for The Morning Walk. Her eyes are failing, so we keep to the same loop on these dawn adventures. (The plan is for her to become so intimately familiar with this route that she will be comfortable traversing it after the light fades from her big brown eyes.)

Sassy and I walk side by side, but our journeys are markedly different. On my end of the leash, concerns center on my to-do list for the day. I make mental notes about work projects, unreturned e-mails, scheduled Zoom meetings, and upcoming appointments. Regrets from the previous day trail me like shadows. I tread, semi-comprehendingly, through the dime-a-dozen Appalachian dawn. In contrast, Sassy remains fully in the present. For her keen senses (smell, hearing, taste), the entire neighborhood has been removed, reprocessed, reshuffled, and hastily replaced over the past twenty-four hours—the weather, the passersby, bird songs from tree branches, scent trails from countless animals, freshly swirled leaves, revised latitudes and longitudes for cars and garbage cans, bits of juicy gossip from her canine associates. Sassy thoroughly investigates any and all changes before dutifully cataloging detailed, site-specific data.

She kicks off each new day by stepping into a new river.

One day last month, Sassy came to an abrupt halt to regard a butterfly she had never met before. I paused, my mental to-do list slipping from my grasp. For a moment, we simply watched: a dog and her human together, marveling at a creature on its own exquisite, fleeting journey.

> *The real voyage of discovery consists not in seeking new landscapes, but in having new eyes.*
>
> —Marcel Proust

THE INTRUSION

This morning found me crossing the Shenandoah Mountains of Virginia. My company car was resolutely crunching its way through the snow and ice as the early morning sun begrudgingly peeked through the roadside rhododendrons.

As I steered into yet another curve, I noticed movement at the edge of the road. A lone bobcat darted from "stage left" ahead of me. With a limp rabbit carcass in its jaws, the cat bounded across the snowy road and then turned to fix me with a malevolent glare.

My car and I were unbidden interlopers in this tableau. My intrusion could not have been more unwelcome or more absolute had I driven through the doors of a cathedral in the midst of an Easter mass.

Uttering my sincerest, most abject apologies, I continued on my way down the mountain.

> *I saw how perfect this situation was, how real, how far beyond my need for comment or justification. All the noises of all the programs, or of all the critics, do nothing to alter this.*
>
> —Thomas Merton

. . . INTO THAT GOOD NIGHT

My quick trip to the store was, quite unexpectedly, transformed into the highlight of my day. In the midst of the Kanawha Street "traffic," I turned my head to regard an older man (late seventies) heading south.

He was perched in the driver's seat of a little blue Honda and (like me) had rolled down his windows in order to relish the mild weather. Also like me, he boasted few functioning hair follicles. His wide grin suggested that he had long since made peace with the betrayal of his hair. Unlike me, this man was full-throatedly and exuberantly singing (warbling?) along to the sounds of the Beach Boys—determinedly attempting to hit the high notes and spectacularly failing in his endeavor, all with the passion of someone who has never questioned whether he should.

His unbridled efforts brought smiles to two mechanics at Steve's Garage . . . and to me as well. Because what was unfolding before us wasn't just a man singing in his car; it was a lesson, a manifesto, a battle cry against the quiet dignity of aging gracefully.

My message to this fine fellow: Keep on rockin' in the free world. Better yet, circle the block and bestow upon me the privilege of accompanying you on your merry adventure. I know all the lyrics to "Wouldn't It Be Nice."

None are so old as those who have outlived enthusiasm.
—Henry David Thoreau

TWO NEW FRIENDS

The morning found me heading south along I-77 in rural Virginia. Due to rain, wind, and fog, I was driving slower than usual, slow enough to catch sight of a lone figure walking on the shoulder of the busy highway. As I drew closer, I focused my attention on the woman as she walked hurriedly and determinedly through the battering elements.

I pondered my options for a brief moment and then pulled my company car off the road just ahead of her. In flagrant disregard of company policy, I asked if I might offer a lift to the wet walker or (at least) call someone for her. Hesitantly, she accepted my offer and climbed into the car and out of the weather.

After thanking me and buckling in, she asked if I could drop her off at the next town (Hillsboro). I unhesitatingly agreed. We began an awkward, halting chat about the day's weather and the endless fields of pumpkins to the east and west. Moments later, and without warning, my passenger broke into uncontrollable sobs. It turned out that she was on the run . . . from an abusive relationship. "He really does love me, I think. There are lots of days when he doesn't hit me." I tiptoed around this minefield carefully, all the while putting miles between her and her point of departure. Attempting to dry her eyes, she remarked, "We don't have kids. I know I need to get away while I can."

When I dropped her off forty minutes later, she assured me that a trusted co-conspirator would arrive soon when the co-conspirator's shift ended. Then my new friend floored me. "Jimmy will be tracking me. Are you traveling from here? Will you take my phone with you?" I teared up and agreed to take her phone.

After dropping off my distraught new friend, I grabbed my own phone and dialed Jeff, a friend of thirty-five years' standing (my previously mentioned ABF) and explained my situation. Together, we formulated a plan.

Some four hours later I pulled into a brightly lit truck stop in North Carolina. After wandering through the bustling oasis of light for a few minutes, I made the acquaintance of a formidable guy named Larry. Explaining my circumstance, I asked Larry if he would take the phone/relay baton with him on the road in the morning. "I'll do you one better. I'll take it with me to Texas and then hand it off to my driving buddy who will be heading north. We're gonna have us some fun with this shit weasel."

How did I choose Larry? I had been privy to his earlier conversation with the truck stop's cashier. He had asked how her kids were doing in school. I knew he was The One—the tone of his voice as much as the content of the conversation.

After entrusting Larry with the phone, I drove a quarter of a mile and stopped my car. I had to process the events of the day. One of many thoughts: Would I have stopped to offer assistance if it had not been raining? After a brief self-examination, I (reproachfully) admitted that I probably would not have.

Into each life, some rain must fall.
—Henry Wadsworth Longfellow

CONTRASTING BUS RIDES

(Note: I have been blessed with the opportunity to rejoin my company's international team on an as-needed basis. Three or four international trips per year? Yes, please!)

Yesterday, I boarded a bus in Ottawa. It was time to cross the Rideau River and take in an afternoon baseball game at Thornton Park. The Ottawa Champions were slated to take on the Sussex Miners.

The day's weather was promising as a city bus arrived at my stop on Catherine Street. An assemblage of local baseball fans with identical afternoon agendas awaited the same bus. The dilemma? Boarding the bus with infinitely patient Canadians. "After you." "Wouldn't think of it." "You were here first, I am sure." "No hurry. Nice day." "Please, I insist." After a considerable delay, the loaded bus was able to depart.

Now, let's go back twenty years. I was visiting ASATC Anne in her newly adopted hometown of Dublin. We were standing in front of the city's bus station, tickets in hand. Our plan? Take the bus westward across the Emerald Isle to Galway. We double-checked our tickets and then ambled over to a deceptively relaxed gathering of fellow would-be travelers. There was lots of good-natured chatting amongst the assembled patrons. Alas, it proved to be the calm before the carnage.

As our bus approached, a marked change in mood overtook the crowd—a suspicious amount of repositioning and donning of leather gloves. When the bus doors opened, we were alarmed to find ourselves at the epicenter of a rugby scrum. The initial forearm shiver to my solar plexus caught me off-guard. The waiting mass of humanity had morphed into Conor McGregor's family reunion.

In retrospect, I'm sure that the Irish have rules for such occasions; it's just that they are few in number. It's roller derby without the rolling. As best I can recall, weapons were not in evidence (noted exception: blood-stained hurling sticks). Ditto for choke holds. I'm fairly sure everything else was *de rigueur*. The spectacle could not have been more intense if the bus in question had advertised Guinness on tap.

A middle-aged English couple was the penultimate duo to climb the bus steps. Distraught and concussed, Anne and I staggered aboard in their wake. Once the final butt (mine) had plopped down on the last remaining seat, the churning chaos ebbed, and everyone abruptly returned to verbal niceties. As we rolled out of the "car park," I glanced back at the bus station. Two triage nurses were calmly prioritizing the casualties. "The ambulances will arrive soon," I convinced myself.

Note to self: Next time you attempt such foolishness, bring along someone who weighs more than 100 pounds.

Note to the reader: The preceding paragraphs may include creative liberties, including a tad of embellishment here and there.

> *In crowds, there is safety in numbers, but also a kind of madness.*
>
> —Friedrich Nietzsche

BIRCH BABY

Last week, I was taking a late-afternoon stroll, wondering and wandering (as I am wont to do). Both processes led me to a small city park perched above Halifax Harbor (Nova Scotia). As I made my way through the park, admiring the trees, the monuments to historical events, and the views of the Norman Rockwell-esque harbor, I was stopped mid-stride by the sight of a young Jewish father reading to his sleeping infant. The two were shaded by a comely paper birch, its protective and enveloping branches swaying in the harbor breeze. I was close enough to watch the infant's tiny chest rise and fall with each breath as the father continued reading aloud. The text was from the Torah, and the young father read the passages in Hebrew—not with an authoritative or pious tone but with a voice that brought back fifty-plus-year-old memories of my mother reading *Winnie-the-Pooh* stories to me as I drifted off to sleep.

I regarded this captivating tableau with affection and awed admiration. In an instant, it manifested the highest aspirations of parenthood, religion, tradition, nature, and all-encompassing love. I yearned to slip my phone from my pocket and snap a single, subtle photo, but I knew that such action would be tantamount to theft, sacrilege, and disrespectful imposition at its most worrisome. Instead, I returned later that evening and retrieved a fallen layer of birch bark to preserve and represent that moment of placid serenity.

> *Train up a child in the way he should go, and when he is old he will not depart from it.*
>
> —Proverbs 22:6 NKJV

LIEUTENANT HOLMAN

Back in the summer, I happened upon *A Sense of the World: How a Blind Man Became History's Greatest Traveler* by Jason Roberts. The enthralling and painstakingly researched book traces and contextualizes the intrepid travels of British Navy Lieutenant James Holman (1786–1857), known to his contemporaries as "The Blind Traveler" (at times in reverence, other times in ridicule) "triumphing not only over blindness but crippling pain, poverty, and the interference of well-meaning authorities."

More than a few of Holman's fellow Royal Geographic Society members questioned Holman's ability to experience (and, as a result, describe and appreciate) far-off lands. One contemporary critic opined, "He might have been in Zanzibar, but how could the Blind Traveler claim to know Zanzibar?"

During and after reading the book, I reflected on my travels, particularly two nights spent in South Africa's Kruger National Park some fifteen years ago.

Eight coworkers and I spent a relaxed weekend within the park's confines, protected from the menagerie of awe-inducing creatures by a 10-foot wall. Each morning and evening, we climbed into Land Rovers and explored the sprawling park (over 7,500 square miles, roughly the combined size of Connecticut and Rhode Island).

We slept in grass-roofed mud huts that featured cold running water and just enough electricity to power a fan and a clock—basic yet magnificent. For decades, I had dreamed of such an experience. My anticipation and expectation had focused (almost entirely) on seeing large, imposing animals. As the weekend played out, the most indelible memories turned out to be the sounds of the night. In almost complete darkness, I would lie in my bed and listen to other-worldly sounds emanating from the surrounding forest. At first, I listened for Large Rumbly Mammals (elephants, rhinos, giraffes, lions, zebras, cape buffaloes), but my attention was soon diverted by calls from the park's nocturnal birds—a cacophony of enchanting, exotic sounds. With no recording device available, I did my best to "catalogue" the calls in my memory for future identification (no such luck).

Over the course of two days, my coworkers and I excitedly filled our checklist of animal sightings: the aforementioned Large Rumbly Animals, wart hogs, crocodiles, oodles of antelopes, and a much-too-close-for-comfort rock python. As exhilarating as these sightings were, they have not crystalized in my memory the way the nocturnal sounds did. I have often read that smell is the sense most closely tied to memory. I'm wondering if hearing would be a close second. I'm thinking that Lieutenant Holman would vote "aye."

> *The only thing worse than being blind is having sight but no vision.*
>
> —Helen Keller

CANADIAN CARTOGRAPHIC ADVENTURE, WEEK ONE

Once again I find myself crisscrossing Canada, our expansive neighbor to the north. I spent much of the day traversing the Trans-Canada Highway from Sault Sainte Marie to Thunder Bay, enjoying occasional teasing glimpses of Lake Superior. The varied landscapes are stunning and will improve considerably in the coming weeks as the native ash, birch, maple, hackberry, and ironwood trees showcase their extravagant, fiery autumnal colors ("colours").

Not for the first time I find myself contemplating Canada: oversized, reserved, self-effacing, tolerant within reason, readily apologetic, reflective, and more than a tad unsure of her place in the world—the nation-state equivalent of yours truly. (Continuing the comparison, growth upon Canada's top is . . . sparse.) Decades ago, a therapist put a thoughtful finger to his chin and stated that I would "make a good Canadian."

If nations took personality tests, Canada would head the list of Type B countries.

In my line of thinking, these realizations are a major reason I eagerly anticipate visiting Canada. On the second night of this particular trip, I sat down and attempted to enumerate my Canadian visits. Over the past forty years, I have visited Canada for several vacations and job assignments. Prior to those adventures were fleeting day trips from my former home in northern Vermont. I have arrived in Canada by airplane, ferry, Volvo, ship, and rail. In pre-9/11 days, I once walked into Quebec from Derby Line, Vermont.

Two of my dogs were born so close to Quebec (in quaint Isle La Motte, Vermont) that they were conversant in French and English.

Spending time in Canada is agreeable and familiar, despite the fact that I have yet to encounter good barbecue or sweet tea, to say nothing of hush puppies, in the land. With notable exceptions for the major cities, I could unhesitatingly adjust to a placid life among the becalmed locals anywhere in the world's second-largest country—well, for eight months out of the year at any rate.

For now, I am content to be abiding in the good graces of the folks here in rural western Ontario. My work is aided by a cross-genre assemblage of Canadian recording artists (Neil Young, Joni Mitchell, Robbie Robertson, The Cowboy Junkies, k.d. lang, The Tragically Hip, Arcade Fire, Gordon Lightfoot, Leonard Cohen) who are content to share space on a USB drive (from whence they entertain me) while I maintain my vigilant watch for wandering moose.

The hush puppies will have to wait.

The world needs more Canada.

—Bono

CANADIAN CARTOGRAPHIC ADVENTURE, WEEK TWO

Half an hour after leaving Ontario and entering the province of Manitoba, the surrounding landscape changed abruptly. An imaginary Forrest Gump, riding shotgun, has been narrating my trip. His perceptive remark upon the boundary crossing: "And just like that, all the trees were gone." We had entered the vast, undulating Canadian prairie.

Later that same day, I stopped to stretch my legs and admire the wide-open horizons. Adjusting my focus, I peered down at the ground beneath my feet. The soil had the texture and color of coffee grounds. "I'll bet even I could grow crops here!"

The following day, I uncharacteristically multi-tasked: I combined my leg stretching with a visit to the men's room at a convenience store. On my way to the toilets, I noticed that every surface in the store was covered in layers of dust. My mind immediately raced back to the 1990s—the undersized general store at Edisto Beach, South Carolina. In those days, my first wife and I often rode our bikes over to the store where we would perform an improvised variation of the scavenger hunt. The object was to see who could find the oldest expiration date on foodstuffs or over-the-counter medications. In my present surroundings, however, the age of the merchandise was not the issue. It was the location of the store (and the time of year). The world outside consisted of nothing but barley fields as far as the eye could see. It was harvest season. A thin veneer of barley dust had blanketed this corner of the world.

My reintroduction to life on the prairie issued forth echoing memories from weeks spent in North Dakota. Throughout my life, I have experienced difficulty judging distances over prairies (or large bodies of water). "Is that cell tower 2 miles from here or 10?" "Is that approaching storm imminent, or will it hit us later tonight?" Manitoba's provincial song should be The Who's "I Can See for Miles."

The unquestioned (and self-indulgent) highlight of my time spent amidst the barley and wheat fields was a long-anticipated stop in Rouleau, Saskatchewan. Canadians far and wide know the town by its other name, "Dog River," from the most popular Canadian sitcom ever, *Corner Gas.* It's the kind of small town where secrets only exist in the abstract, and the corner gas station, for all intents, functions as the town square. It's where the humor flows easily and quasi-familial coziness lingers unhindered.

Dog River is to Canadians what Mayberry is to small-town America, only with hockey and curling references and more self-deprecating quips. The eight main characters never take themselves too seriously, regularly taking time to mull over life's little quirks over coffee and sandwiches. It is television at its finest: small-town wisdom served with a wink—biggest thumbs up I can offer.

Since it was Sunday, I was relishing both the rare day off and the sunny disposition of the town's residents. The sole employee of Rouleau's post office was a fountain of information on both the show and the history of the town. We chatted amiably and unhurriedly, comparing and contrasting Mayberry/Mount Airy and Dog River/Rouleau. Her parting words were, "If you find yourself back in town, stop by the house. My husband and I live in the little gray house across the street from Oscar and Emma's place."

On Monday, my coworker and I turned our car back to the east in order to update the road networks in and around Manitoba's lone city: Winnipeg. When our working hours come to an end, we spend our time exploring a "controlled environment" within the city—an extensive network of tunnels, enclosed corridors, and elevated, glassed-in walkways—all designed for pedestrians. This network is insulated from the brutal winters (a major bonus) and envied by the area's burgeoning prairie dog populations.

In my estimation, the most impressive network of (Canadian) winterized passageways belongs to Montreal. For all intents and purposes, you can get anywhere in the city using walkways, tunnels, and subways without ever having to knock the snow from your boots. The network is a marvel in civil and transportation engineering. I could spend a winter in Montreal wearing only jeans and short-sleeved shirts (though by March I would likely be suffering from Subterranean Homesick Blues). But who knows? I might even learn a few French phrases along the way. At present, the best I can offer is "Chevrolet, *s'il vous plait*."

> *You [Canada] are a big country. You are the kindest country in the world. You are like a really nice apartment over a meth lab.*
>
> —Robin Williams

BLUE RIDGE PARADOX

I have been updating maps in the Blue Ridge Mountains of North Carolina this week. Much of my work—in essence, all of it—involves location-based data (LBD). I have been co-processing LBD with LBM (location-based memories) for this particular project.

It would and does seem that every named town or hamlet on my map overflows with LBM: Tryon, Hendersonville, Bryson City, Lake Junaluska, Blowing Rock, Rutherfordton, Cherokee, Maggie Valley, Swannanoa, Banner Elk, Brevard, Bat Cave, Lake Lure. As I drive, James Earl Jones' voice echoes, "The memories will be so thick, they'll have to brush them away from their faces."

Needless to state, my chronic, all-encompassing sentimentality is frequently my undoing.

As I attempt to focus on the work at hand, my thoughts fluctuate between the present and the past—distracted driving. I hear the ghost of Asheville's Thomas Wolfe remind me that I can't go home again. A young black bear's glance before disappearing into morning mist and staghorn sumac tells me otherwise. The kitschy, handmade sign at the door of the craft shop commands me to "Bloom where you are planted." The frustrated botanist within me counters with arguments about soil structure and composition. What are the sublethal effects and stresses of a compromised transplanting effort?

The torrent of memories continues. The innumerable benevolences bestowed, the opportunities foregone, the connections made and lost. Supporting cast members, named and unnamed, who left their indelible imprints. The guiding, reassuring hands of departed adults now taking rest from their labors of love. Joyfully rediscovered friends from decades past. Holy Ground in the form of rivers, hills, houses, waterfalls, and shady lanes. Fleeting, shimmering glimpses of familiar spring birds. Taken together, a veritable host of stimuli coalesce into atmospheric comfort food.

Words that have been my companions for the week: dwell, linger, pause.

The paradox of cherished memories . . . I seek them, and they bring smiles—smiles that inevitably lead to wistfulness. After turning to leave the site of a particularly blessed memory, I thought of Robert Frost: "Yet knowing how way leads on to way, I doubted if I should ever come back."

> *Only the paradox comes anywhere near to comprehending the fullness of life.*
>
> —Carl Jung

WAVES OF EMOTION

Today I returned home from a frenzied week at Myrtle Beach. Scores of well-documented, photographed memories provide digital evidence of our time there. My most significant memory was not saved for posterity in a snapshot or a video on my phone. It has been securely lodged in the core of my being.

My six-year-old grandson and I were standing in 1.5 feet of water, splashing and dodging in the waves. It would not be possible for me to overstate this milestone. On previous trips, William would cautiously allow the ocean water to cover his tiny feet—his ankles on particularly adventurous days.

The excursion into the waves brought back memories of my own grandfather, an Old Salt, gently coaxing me into the ocean a scant 10 miles from that very spot but a sobering fifty-five years ago. In a kaleidoscope of perspectives, the decades blurred. I was young, and I was old. I was the boy. I was the grandpa. I was everything and everyone in between.

In the blink of an eye, my life's frenetic, incongruous complexity faded into man, boy, waves.

After the first few waves hit us, my grandson slowly became aware of a certainty. The stars might become preoccupied and forget to shine. Mice might begin to chase cats. But although "Poppy" was by no means the strongest person on the beach, there was no way he was going to let go of the top of that little swim vest. Trust is akin to grace. It is a benevolent gift not to be taken lightly.

At this point in his young life, the boy may or may not realize that I am not his biological grandfather, that I had come into the family picture a scant five years before his joy-filled arrival. In the years ahead, genetics may or may not matter to him. I only know I couldn't love that little fellow more.

> *Because there's nothing more beautiful than the way the ocean refuses to stop kissing the shoreline, no matter how many times it's sent away.*
>
> —Sarah Kay

REFLECTIONS ON A DAY'S END, LATITUDE 55.43

One month ago I was standing on the starboard deck of an immense ferry as it set sail from a Swedish port under cover of night en route to a Polish dock some eight hours to the south. Echoes of 100-year-old sailing stories from my seafaring grandfather found me.

One hour beforehand, I had been displaying my ticket and passport to the terminal's attendant. As she examined my passport, I noticed that her head tilted to one side; a curious expression accompanied the movement. She double-checked my papers and replied that in her five years at her present post, she had never seen an American passport. In perfect English, she added that she hoped I had enjoyed my stay in Sweden. In reply, I earnestly related that I had, indeed. As I drove up the loading ramp, I surmised that most Americans take the faster (by an order of magnitude) option of flight. I suppressed a grin as I regarded myself a bit more of an explorer and, perhaps, a bit less of a herded sheep.

I stood on the ferry's deck for a solid hour, gripping the polished wood of the handrail and bidding a forlorn farewell to an adventurous day off in the sleepy harbor town of Ystad. As I marveled at the perfection of both night and town, I paused to locate lights from the stately train station, the town museum, the nineteenth-century theater, the marina, the sailors' chandlery, the brick water tower, the regal Continental Hotel—all points of interest that ASATC Anne and I had investigated during the course of the long summer's day. The lights pled their case together: "Here we are in all our finery. Are you quite sure you are content to sail away?" At one point, I turned my head westward at the sound of a train's whistle. I commented to myself, "Ah, the evening train from Malmö" with the certainty and assured familiarity of a local.

Appreciation for the town and the wistfulness of having to leave it behind battled for supremacy in my quasi-gelatinous state. I struggled with the knowledge that a smorgasbord of the town's hidden gems had been left undiscovered. Slighted hollyhocks. Weathered, half-timbered houses left unappreciated. Pastries unnibbled. Cherubic children unsmiled upon. Memories of Ystad enveloped by the gathering night sky and the calm Baltic Sea lingered.

Alongside the allure of the exotic was and is the realization that this chronic longing is not just for a physical place. It's for revelations of novelty—the thrill of a new beginning, the challenge of adaptation accompanied by anticipation that comes from embracing the unfamiliar.

As I reflect on the endless virtues of this pleasingly unassuming town, I'm reminded that life in all its complexity and uncertainty is a journey that extends beyond the boundaries of what I know (or what I think I know). This realization serves as a catalyst, propelling me forward and encouraging me to take steps toward the unknown.

Any voyage of discovery is incomplete without an accompanying discovery of . . . self.

> *Man cannot discover new oceans without first losing sight of the shore.*
>
> —Andre Gide

SIXTY-STEP PROGRAM ON COMPASSION

A few hours ago, my coworker and I stopped for dinner at a Greek restaurant located across from the train station in Szczecin, Poland. Just as we were laying claim to a table on the broad sidewalk, I noticed a conservatively dressed elderly couple in front of the train station. They were standing close together by an ancient wooden easel, handing out Jehovah's Witnesses literature. I avoided any possible eye contact and focused on my menu.

Nearly an hour later, after greedily devouring my chicken souvlaki, I noticed that the JW couple was on the move, easel and pamphlets in hand. They tottered past our table and began what I surmised was part of their nightly ritual, managing to get themselves and their unwieldy cargo up sixty or so steep granite steps.

As they braced themselves at the base of the steps, I hesitated.

I uncharitably discounted the pair. "Wacko religious fanatics."

After my humbling hesitation, I caught (and kicked) myself. How many of my acquaintances would see me in that same harsh light? I rose from my chair and headed toward the couple, catching up with them on the second step, assisting them for the next fifty-eight.

It was a day filled with sights of glorious, ancient buildings and undulating fields of Polish wheat. Now I am lying in bed thinking of those surprised and appreciative folks, and the stark contrast with the unvarnished ugliness of my hesitation.

Doubtless, my lesson for the day.

We should model the kindness we want to see.

—Brené Brown

DZIADEK CONNECTION IN LODZ

My post-dinner routine during my two weeks in Poland included, without fail, exploratory nightly walks—walks that sought out history, architecture, nature, street art, dogs, and whimsy . . . but also human connections. After many successive nights, I found that I have become almost numb to sixteenth-century grandeur. People? That is quite another story. A few blocks away from the regal, bustling town squares, I have, with regularity found neighborhoods comprised of battered apartment buildings—places that house the capable workforce for the shops, restaurants, bars, hotels, and other businesses. I enjoy seeking out the backbone of society, the people who (as chronicler George Bailey heatedly remarks every December) "do most of the working and paying and living and dying" in the community.

On Monday and Tuesday of this week, I worked in the city of Lodz, a pre-war textile manufacturing hub. Judging by the countless abandoned factories on the outskirts of town, I thought Lodz might provide me with one of the remaining items on my Polish Scavenger Hunt list: an old Soviet-made

Lada. I struck out there but did stumble upon a beleaguered, blue Yugo in a long- neglected vacant lot. The rusted heap was missing one door and its rear axle. I commented to myself that the car stood as much of a chance of reassemblage as its namesake.

On Tuesday night, I happened upon a boisterous group of small children in one of Lodz's many neighborhood parks. The high-pitched chorus of laughs reached my ears long before I caught sight of the frolicking children nestled in a circle. The activity was as familiar as the dialogue was unfamiliar. "*Kaczka, kaczka, kaczka, kaczka . . . gęś*!" A grin found its way to my face as context allowed for quick translation: "Duck, duck, duck, duck, GOOSE!"

I found a low cement wall and settled in to take in the merriment. As I sat and enjoyed the proceedings, child after child rose to accept his or her turn to encircle the assemblage of laughing children. However, I soon discovered that the watcher was being watched. A couple of older men on the opposite side of the park were eyeing me with suspicion. The look on their faces let me know that I had pinged on their Stranger Danger radar. "Community Watch."

Cautiously, I walked toward the men, who stood as I approached. They aimed a few pointed questions in my direction. In response, I lamely replied, "*Nie Polska*." I pensively waited while they processed this bit of information. As I met their appraising gazes, I reached for my cell phone. Within a few seconds, I had located a couple of photos featuring me with my three grandchildren. I emphatically put my hand over my heart. The message was received. "*Dziadek*!" As I struggled to make sense of the word, the two men pointed to each other and then to me. "*Dziadek*!" I smiled at the communal connection. We were all grandfathers.

We sat together and enjoyed a few minutes of companionable silence watching the energetic children at play. The older of the two men looked at me and then pointed a gnarled finger at the children. "Is good." In response, I beamed. "*Tak*! *Tak*! Is good!"

I stood to take my leave, stopping to shake the hands of my fellow *dziadeks*. My thoughts turned to Will Rogers: "A stranger is just a friend I haven't met yet." I followed this with a phrase of my own: "What divides us diminishes us."

> *My grandfather was a wonderful role model. Through him I got to know the gentle side of men.*
>
> —Sarah Long

THE EXIT RAMP

As I made my way south along the Virginia section of I-81 last week, I pondered—hardly a surprise as this is the default setting for sentimental, nostalgic persons. My thoughts ventured back to my first journey on I-81 the summer of 1989. I was leaving Georgia for my new home in Vermont (with a scheduled stop in Cooperstown, New York).

As I reminisced on that transformative journey, I took notice of a car in my rearview mirror. The driver looked to be a few years older than I and was keeping pace in his 1990s vintage navy blue Buick. Ten minutes or so later, I again caught him in my mirror. Like me, he appeared to be in no hurry and seemed to be admiring the countryside. For all I knew, he too was listening to Roberta Flack and Donny Hathaway.

My "shadow" (I dubbed him "Billy" because he looked like a Billy) followed right along behind me for over an hour before veering—without warning, permission, or submitted flight plan—toward the exit ramp to Highway 220. Just like that, my happenstance traveling companion unceremoniously disappeared, called away by an emptying gas tank or the Cracker Barrel sign.

A friend at my home church reminds me from time to time to "Quit Taking It Personally" ("Q-TIP"), sage words from a wise man. He (and countless others) knows that I tend to take things, all manner of things, personally. I smiled at the remembrance of his considered counsel. Not even I would leap to the conclusion that I had somehow caused the aforementioned highway separation. Billy (a Calvinist?) had arrived on my radar with a pre-determined destination that day—his own journey to complete.

Those thoughts led me to reflect on the countless number of people who have entered my life only to, days or decades later, venture toward their respective exit ramps. During and after those separations, I find myself ensnared by my recurring personal quandary of "What did I do or say?" I berate and question myself; I critically assess my behavior. My mind becomes a minefield of insecurities. Sigh. "I wasn't _________ enough." "What did I do to deserve radio silence?" Ah, the debilitating (though universal) human experience of saying goodbye. If I were an Old Testament figure, significant partings in my life would doubtless reduce me to weeping, wailing, and gnashing of teeth—perhaps even the rending of garments.

Accepting the fact that all relationships are fluid is a work in progress for me. Relationships ebb and flow, and sometimes they drift into quiet corners of memory.

How incalculably easier it is for me to understand a turn signal and a geographic destination than it is for me to grasp why an acquaintance might have shared my "lane" for a while, only to veer away. I must navigate the messy terrain of emotions and accept that their journey is not mine; their horizon is not mine. A healthier me must pause and wish them Godspeed.

I continue to work on Q-TIP, along with my sense of appreciation and gratitude for past, present, and future fellow travelers.

> *Farewell has a sweet sound of reluctance. Good-by is short and final, a word with teeth sharp to bite through the string that ties past to the future.*
>
> —John Steinbeck

MEN AT WORK

From my office here at home, I bore witness as two men struggled to collect our garbage in the midst of a downpour. As I sat and watched these men at work, my mind was filled with thoughts of Echol Cole and Robert Walker—two sanitation workers who, due to the color of their skin, were denied entrance to the city's sanitation offices and were left to seek shelter in the back of a garbage truck. Memphis 1968. (The compactor malfunctioned in the rain, killing both men.)

After this visit to the past, I returned to my task at hand: updating a land-use map of Woodstock, Ontario. Only I didn't. My thoughts returned to the men collecting garbage in my otherwise quiet neighborhood. My hands abandoned their cartographic duties and found themselves in my lap.

My work environment? My ergonomic chair. A dry, well-lit room, 72 degrees. My faithful, four-legged cohort contentedly napping on the floor next to me. The Brooklyn Duo playing Pachelbel's "Canon in D" in the background. As I continued to assess my situation, I realized that I did not know (and indeed did not care) if any of the doors to my house were locked.

I paused to offer my most solemn attempt at silent prayer for the town's sanitation workers—prayers for comfort and safety.

My many blessings go unrecognized and underappreciated on most days. Shame.

> *The dignity of work is not measured by the work itself but by the man who does it.*
>
> —*Booker T. Washington*

"IN-BETWEENS" OF ROW 11

Amy and I were firmly ensconced in Row 11 during yesterday's two-hour flight. It was an assignment in more ways than one.

In rows 9 and 10 sat an unassuming, deferential, clear-eyed, unobtrusive Mennonite family: mother, father, three teen daughters, and a tween son. They spoke in hushed tones, rested silently, and shared homemade snacks contentedly.

Behind me, in Row 12, sat two grey-haired men in their fifties. When the collection of passengers boarded the plane, the two men were strangers. Over the course of the two-hour flight, they struck up a friendship based on common interests and experiences.

In a combined and concerted effort, the two self-viewed Captains of Industry covered in excruciating detail their burgeoning careers; their irrational ex-wives; and their own hapless, feckless, entitled children, all with the reverberating decibel levels and subtlety of two-stroke chainsaws. I dubbed the two men Randolph and Mortimer.

Mortimer weighed in on his ex-wife: "Doesn't have the sense that God gave a goat. You know, when she left me, she took up with a guy from our factory floor. Twelve-dollar-an-hour guy. Steel-toed boots, metal lunch pail, the whole works" (protracted laugh). Randolph rejoined with similar details. "I don't know how my wife ever got her degree. Her brains are in her bra."

The ensuing comments on their children—their own children—were no more charitable. The coarse words hung heavily in the air of the cabin for all to hear. Randolph's eldest had spent four years at an elite prep school. "All he got was the ability to cuss me out in French." Mortimer's daughter had shown potential at one point but had ended up heading out West to "find herself." "These days, she looks like a Jamaican street vendor." Both sets of offspring, it would seem, had proven themselves to be categorically incapable of following sage, fatherly advice.

The deluge of details regarding Randolph and Mortimer's comparable rises to financial prominence and opulent decadence was less grating but just as revealing. At one point, Mortimer gleefully recalled the day he deftly out-maneuvered an eighty-two-year-old landowner. "Had the sap over a barrel."

I offered silent thanks that Amy and I had been stationed between the lions and the lambs. We functioned as a makeshift buffer at 30,000 feet, a breakwater between the tumultuous sea and the placid harbor.

My respective seating position gave me pause—an apt metaphor for my life between contrasting reference points. (What, pray tell, is a cartographer without reference points?) My sixty-plus years have been spent between the gated community and the projects, between the big city and the hamlet, between the in crowd and the outcasts, between Nieman Marcus and Big Lots, between the zealot and the agnostic, between the proud and the pitied, between the mill owner's son and the millworker's son, between confidence and confoundedness, between the devil and the deep blue sea.

A life lived in the in-betweens—how much of this has been by design? How much of my existence has been defined or confined by a murky cocktail of expectation, accountability, and conformity? Have I unconsciously set my own boundaries and limits? Have I allowed others to do so?

Am I seeking and finding smug self-assurance by steadfastly coloring within the lines while unknowingly resting within a carefully delineated comfort zone?

When I was a kid, I was convinced that I would have all of this worked out by age sixteen at the very latest.

> *Happiness is not a matter of intensity but of balance, order, rhythm, and harmony.*
>
> —*Thomas Merton*

TWO WEEKS, TWO DRIVERS, TWO CATHEDRALS

Here in Guadalajara, I have been blessed with two personable, conscientious, affable, and dependable drivers: Edgar for week one and Manny for week two. The two men are retired police officers who, as it turned out, have been friends since grade school. Though language was a barrier (my last Spanish class was in 1978, the year Cervantes completed *Don Quixote*), we were able to exchange basic messages effectively, if a bit clumsily—lots of hand motions along with liberal use of Google Translate.

After working with Edgar for two days, I was invited to join him for the early mass at the venerable Guadalajara Cathedral (sixteenth century). I readily agreed, with full knowledge that the service would be offered in Latin and Spanish. Treasured revelations transcend language. After the service, I treated Edgar to brunch as he patiently answered my questions about the cathedral and the morning's service.

After dinner last night, Manny (this week's driver) and I escaped the traffic of the city. As previously arranged, Manny drove me to his childhood home, a farm located an hour's drive to the west. Though Manny lives in Guadalajara, his two brothers continue to run the family farm, growing beans, soybeans, and corn throughout the year. For the last third of our drive, we meandered through a maze of dusty, winding, and signless roads, easing past a handful of villages that were being shuttered for the night.

The brothers, Carlos and Javier, welcomed us to the farm with (quite literally) open arms. *¡El niño pródigo de la ciudad regresa!* ("The prodigal city boy returns!"). Curious children and farm dogs emerged from the darkness that gathered around the expansive barn. Moments later, the wives greeted us at the farmhouse door.

After the good-natured, teasing welcoming of their big city brother, the family turned its attention to me. I was ceremoniously elevated from road-weary gringo to Visiting Dignitary—a royal greeting. Their collective fuss over my arrival was, quite paradoxically, humbling.

After a brief visit to the house, I walked with Manny and Javier to a battered but unbowed GMC pickup. The plan was to drive up to a rocky outcrop in the farmland's midst. Manny had chosen this particular night due to the serendipitous combination of a new moon and a forecast for a calm, cloudless night. We were going star-gazing. Two of Javier's grandsons earnestly recited a list of reasons why they should be allowed to join us but were sternly guided back to the house. Two of the farm dogs would not be dissuaded and proceeded to trot along the inclining dirt road, serving as guides and lookouts.

At about 5,800 feet, our vantage point had been chosen for its 360-degree views: mountainous horizon to mountainous horizon. As I turned my eyes toward the heavens, my breath was abruptly taken from me. The sharp contrasts, the staggering panorama, the inky black canvas, the palpable stillness all demanded reverence. After a few minutes, the dogs perked up their ears in response to intermittent conversations of coyotes and owls.

I mimicked the actions of the two brothers and stretched out flat on my back. (A passing Chinese spy balloon could have mistaken us for a large Mercedes-Benz emblem.) The three of us maintained a solemn, companionable silence for what seemed like ten minutes. Later, I would learn we had spent more than thirty minutes on our backs, taking in the splendor. After witnessing the evening's pageantry, Manny, Javier, and I emitted an off-key chorus of age-appropriate grunting noises as we struggled to our feet. I remarked and gestured to Javier that if I were to take up residence on their farm, I would retreat to that vantage point for each and every new moon—and some full moons.

We drove slowly back to the farmhouse where an assemblage of family members once again met us. Carlos and his wife produced a bottle of (local) tequila and gestured for me to partake. After the briefest of hesitations, I nodded and accepted my shot glass. How, especially on this night and in this place, could I deny their traditional, heartfelt hospitality and attempt to detail the tragedy-filled personal history behind my teetotaler status? Unthinkable. In response to their gracious gesture, I offered entertainment as my newfound friends bore witness to my teary, gasping reaction to a torched esophagus.

In a joyous mixture of conviviality, appreciation, and tequila, Manny and I said our goodbyes and headed back to our car. On the drive back to Guadalajara, my mind recalled and pondered the writings of Emerson.

> *If the stars should appear one night in a thousand years, how would men believe and adore; and preserve for many generations the remembrance of the City of God which had been shown! But every night come out these envoys of beauty, and light the universe with their admonishing smile.*
>
> —Ralph Waldo Emerson

EMPLOYEE EVALUATION

With *beaucoups* gratitude for the many people involved, Amy and I have welcomed Emmy the border collie to our fold. Lots of kind-hearted folks were instrumental in getting her to and from a foster mom in Virginia. From there, faithful friends went to bat for us, assuring the rescue organization that we would provide a suitable, loving home for the displaced, disoriented (but zealously affectionate) pooch.

Emmy has big shoes to fill as my coworker, taking over for the dearly departed Sassy. In keeping with her breed's reputation, Emmy has proven to be a quick study. Her learning curve for the basics of cartography has been extraordinary. Ten days into her new position, she already possesses a firm grasp of the geographic coordinate system, as well as spherical-image-projection options. She even purged obsolete folders from my FTP site, freeing up space for new data.

In her free time, she has taken on the task of bringing order to the chaos that is the recalcitrant, incorrigible squirrel population at the local college. In the offing? A weekend position: Herder of Boisterous Grandchildren.

On our frequent neighborhood patrols, she steadfastly assumes her mantle of sounding board. A keen listener, she brings a wealth of understanding to my tales of incomprehension, loss, and vulnerability. With impeccable gentility, she listens to my musings, ideas, philosophies, and aspirations, all the while keeping a straight face.

For her initial evaluation, I am giving her 7 stars (on a scale of 1–5).

> *He is your friend, your partner, your defender, your dog. You are his life, his love, his leader. He will be yours, faithful and true, to the last beat of his heart. You owe it to him to be worthy of such devotion. . . . Our dogs will love and admire the meanest of us, and feed our colossal vanity with their uncritical homage.*
>
> —Agnes Repplier

RECONNECTING WITH ANDY

For all of my complaining about Facebook, I must say that it performs an invaluable service: keeping up with a cross-section of friends and acquaintances from the fifteen towns I have called home.

Last month, a mutual friend reconnected me with a neighbor from my childhood, a friend who desperately needed reconnection. Andy and his family have been through the proverbial wringer over the past six months.

After an exchange of e-mails, Andy gave me his cell phone number. On Wednesday night, I found myself in conversation with him for the first time in fifty years (to the month). After a quick "catch up," Andy haltingly related the series of events that had devastated his family.

In December, Andy (and Carol) received word that their daughter, Sherry, had miscarried in the early days of her third trimester. Overwhelmed by a deluge of heartache and misplaced guilt, Sherry left her job and sought solace in isolation and self-medication.

By February, she had stopped eating and only slept in abbreviated, fitful stretches. By March, she had cut off communication with everyone except her pleading parents. Sherry thwarted all attempts at intervention, denying everyone access to her apartment.

One week before Mother's Day, Sherry ventured out to her car in the dark of night. Alone, she drove to the parking lot of the hospital where she had lost her son. Sitting behind her steering wheel, she wrote a short note to her parents, stating that since her son could not be with her, she would go to him. Sherry then locked her car and overdosed on a cocktail of prescription meds beneath a parking-lot streetlight.

Andy and Carol don't need answers from me. They need opportunities to share this oppressive burden.

After the phone call, it was time for me to process, something I do slowly. I have found that walking usually helps, so I pulled on my sneakers, snapped the leash on Emmy's collar, and took a walk around my neighborhood.

Countless thoughts and memories have found their way to me. One recurring, convicting thought is that the people I encounter lead largely unknown lives that may very well be careening through unknown and unfathomable turmoil and traumas—the retail clerk, the waitress, that "road-rage" guy, the unfriendly neighbor, the caustic coworker.

Today served as a sharp reminder for me: pause and consider.

> *The most precious gift we can offer anyone is our attention.*
>
> —*Thich Nhat Hanh*

ANDY'S ADDENDUM

Throughout the ensuing months, I kept tabs on Andy, doing my level best to offer encouragement, mostly via e-mail. About a year after Sherry's death, a frustrated Andy sent me an e-mail, a message filled with vexation. "I have had it up to here with lectures and pep talks from my coworkers and neighbors. I really need a friend who can recognize when it's time to stop dishing out unsolicited advice, someone who will just help me breathe."

Local "friends" had been delivering what Andy referred to as "The Seven Words Guaranteed to End a Friendship." The words that had been assaulting Andy's ears? "You should be over that by now." Sigh. Callous "friends" had stuck the knife in and then proceeded to twist the handle. I replied to Andy's message with all the empathy and understanding I could muster.

Then I sat at my desk for long minutes, scratching Emmy's head and wondering aloud at a thought process that would lead anyone, especially a friend, to proclaim such caustic words.

CHANCE ENCOUNTER WITH AN EMPTY HEART

Another week on the road. Last night found me in Cincinnati, the city that once decided "Jerry Springer should be our mayor."

Earlier tonight, I stepped through the door of a busy restaurant. While perusing a posted menu, I took notice of a man with carefully cropped white hair as he painstakingly rose from a bench seat in the waiting area. In the process, he disconnected what I surmised was a disheartening phone call. As the man rose, a leather wallet fell from his lap and softly plopped on the carpeted floor, undetected.

When the man turned to make his way to the cheery hostess, I circled behind and retrieved the wallet. The man was in the process of requesting a table for one as I tentatively tapped him on the shoulder. "Excuse me, but it seems you left something behind." The man's face registered a brief, absent-minded look of confusion followed by a spark of self-admonishing clarity. "Oh, my. Thank you, thank you. I'm afraid my mind was far away."

Visibly flustered, he shook his head and awkwardly repeated his thanks. "Are you here with someone?" he asked. "Would you care to join me? It's my treat. The least I can do." Rather unconvincingly, I declined the offer. "Oh, it was nothing," I said. "I just happened to see it fall as you stood up." The man repeated his entreaty. "Really, I would appreciate it. You'd be doing me a great favor. Another favor." I acquiesced.

The man introduced himself as Harold and then politely asked the hostess for a table for two. On the way to our table, Harold informed me that the man he had planned to meet had just phoned with a last-minute dinner cancellation. "Work, it would seem. The very thing I wanted to talk to him about."

Harold had entered retirement just as COVID hit and was having trouble adjusting to Life Beyond Work. As our meal progressed, Harold divulged his cautionary tale. "I succeeded in business (corporate risk-management) but failed spectacularly in my personal life. My devotion—no, my obsession with work came at the expense of my personal life. Balance? There was none. Even when I was spending time with my family I was usually preoccupied with some aspect of work. When e-mails and then smartphones came along, the wheels really came off—divorce followed by disconnection with my adult children. That Harry Chapin song about the cat and the cradle? Bingo."

In actuality, his story brought to mind a Warren Zevon song, "Empty Hearted Town," perhaps due to the setting—night falling on a big city during the early days of autumn.

Every lilting word of the ballad reflected Harold's mournful story. Just replace L.A. with Cincinnati.

Over the course of the meal, Harold would interrupt his tale to gauge my response or ask one or two obligatory questions about my life. However, I was keenly aware that my role for the night was to serve as a listener. In this assigned role, I sensed Harold's deep-seated angst and did my level best to stay present and invested.

Harold informed me that he had spent the last two days with an estranged son in Michigan and that the reunion had not gone well. "Unqualified disaster. Unqualified disaster." Harold was now headed south to his retirement home in Florida, having stopped in Cincinnati with plans to dine with a protégé of sorts in hopes that he might discourage the younger man from following in Harold's path. "Ah, listen to me! I must sound like the Ghost of Christmas Past."

We sat and talked for over an hour—no pretense, no filter, no small talk, no politics.

I asked about Harold's retirement village in Florida. "Are there folks in your neighborhood who share common interests? Any similar stories there?" Harold unhesitatingly nodded. "Oh yes, tons. But they don't seem to struggle with regrets the way I do. A round of golf and a stiff drink seem to fix whatever might be troubling them."

After a moment of pondering, Harold offered, "But maybe that's what I don't need. Maybe it isn't helpful for me to be amongst people who are, in many ways, the person that I am. Maybe I need to look for a place comprised of people who are like the person I want to become." That notion, that idea, that possibility seemed to hit Harold like a bolt out of the blue, and for the first time that night, Harold smiled.

After dinner, Harold and I walked out of the restaurant together. I thanked him for both the meal and the conversation; in return, he stopped to look me in the eye. "You know what I will miss when I get home on Friday? When I pull into my little driveway in Florida, I won't have anyone to call to say that I made it home." "Wrong," I replied. I handed him my business card. "Call me. I really want to know that you made it home okay."

I climbed in my car and thought to myself, "Who knows? Sometimes little things can be big things."

> *Each man is a half-open door leading to a room for everyone.*
>
> —Tomas Tranströmer

WIDE-OPEN THROTTLE

I have spent the better part of the past two weeks with my sister's family in South Carolina. My four-year-old great-nephew and my two-year-old great-niece provided live entertainment.

The four-year-old features a ready, winning smile. He is the inquisitive and contemplative one, focusing much of his attention on excavators and dinosaurs. In marked contrast, the two-year-old is a hummingbird in human form. Her waking hours are spent zooming from shiny object to shiny object with a compelling, hair-on-fire sense of urgency. She is the smallest child in her preschool class, but she more than makes up for it with her frenetic, feverish level of activity.

She loves running circles around the kitchen island, perpetually curious about what might be happening around the next corner. Last Tuesday, I stood in awed silence as I watched the family's two labradoodles join her in this pursuit. I was filled with bemusement, especially at one particular moment during the hell-for-leather chase when she found herself (very temporarily) in third place. She erased the deficit by darting ahead, utilizing her tiny elbows to jostle her way back into the lead. In so doing, she reminded me of nothing so much as The World's Smallest (and most determined) Roller Derby Queen.

> *You don't stop laughing when you grow old, you grow old when you stop laughing.*
>
> —George Bernard Shaw

EMMY, CAN YOU HEAR ME?

Some nine months ago, Emmy the border collie agreed to adopt me. She has unquestionably been a welcomed presence in our midst.

Within the last month, we have encountered an unexpected development. Emmy is losing her hearing—rapidly. These days, her ears only respond to loud, sharp noises. (On a related note, Emmy knows when the three-year-old granddaughter comes to pay a visit.)

Over the past week, and quite possibly in vain, I have made a conscious effort to tell her several nice things each day, holding my head close to hers and using a loud (but what I hope is a soothing and unconcerned) voice. During this time, I have also noticed that (more than ever) she feels the need to have me in her sight.

Like her eight predecessors, Emmy has quickly become my steadfast keeper of secrets, the long-suffering recipient of countless puns and wince-inducing plays on words—my Walk or Die. On this very morning, we reached a tacit understanding. My torrent of stream-of-consciousness words will continue. She will continue to hold my confidence and trust as my need to unburden myself will doubtless continue unabated. She will take this duty, along with her new limitation, in her graceful stride.

Addendum: The following morning, I looked out on our backyard and noticed Emmy's footprints through last night's snow. Circuitous route! (It brought to mind Billy from *Family Circus.*) The meandering path brought the realization that Emmy and I still have countless new adventures ahead of us.

> *Kindness is a language which the deaf can hear and the blind can see.*
>
> —Mark Twain

CÓRDOBA, SPAIN

Near the end of tonight's stroll around the 2,800-year-old city of Córdoba, I stopped just short of my hotel to park myself on a park bench.

After a pleasant few moments of people-watching, I was joined by a smartly dressed, angular, silver-haired man with a rather stylish cane. (Think Andalusian James Coburn.) He began our chat in Spanish but quickly and effortlessly switched to English.

In short order, I would learn that my new friend was a retired history professor . . . and a widower. We unhurriedly swapped stories in the fading half-light, pausing periodically for pleasantries with an assortment of his passing amigos.

I asked the good-natured fellow a few questions about the city's long history—the Romans, the Moors, the Spanish Inquisition, and more. He, in turn, provided me with a ten-minute "TED Talk" on the subject.

He then moved on, unprodded, to more recent history. "For Spain, the twentieth century was all but nonstop political power grabs—coups and attempted coups, Spaniards killing

Spaniards, year after year, decade after decade. We didn't even pause to choose sides for the two world wars, just the continued fighting of faction versus faction. Allegiances forged, only to be broken—every economic class, every political leaning. Was the church in the mix? Bet your last dollar. It's a travesty when one's ideology becomes more important than the life of one's neighbor."

Upon that sage reflection, he gazed into the distance, grabbed his cane, and bid me a pleasant evening.

> *I would sooner be a foreigner in Spain than in most countries. How easy it is to make friends in Spain!*
>
> —George Orwell

GRANADA, SPAIN

For the past two nights I have slept in a seventeenth-century monastery. In the 1980s, the building was painstakingly renovated, updated, and repurposed as a hotel. The entire structure is a marvel, complete with two enclosed courtyards, a maze of arched corridors, and zillions of hand-painted tiles.

My room features two windows, one facing the snow-capped Sierra Nevadas and the other facing the city of Granada. An attached building, centuries newer, houses a Catholic school. The hotel and school share a common entryway opposite a river bridge built by the Romans.

Yesterday morning and again this morning I spent considerable time perched in my company car, busily connecting various pieces of electronic mapping equipment to my laptop. It is an involved process, demanding a good fifteen minutes of repositioning and double-checking the web of cables. This morning, I smiled as I remembered a comment made by a coworker some twenty years ago as we fumbled through the identical process: "Mary Jo Kopechne would never be able to get out of this car!"

For entertainment during setup, my current coworker and I have taken to watching the cavalcade of school children as they march toward the school's front door. With our car windows up (and a language barrier), we have missed out on the accompanying conversations.

Not to be thwarted, we studied the body language of students and parents—who is mad at whom, who had absentmindedly left home without his or her "Ride or Cry" stuffed animal, who was experiencing difficulty in the waking process (and who was rip-roaring ready to go), who was running behind schedule, who was (at least on that day) patient, who could be trusted to find the way to the front door, who was easily distracted from the task at hand, who welcomed (and who shied away from) hugs and kisses, and on and on.

As we sat watching, one purple-clad, pig-tailed five-year-old (upon parental bidding) put her head, shoulders—the entirety of her tiny body—into an emphatic, prolonged nose-blowing. She then turned to commit this same diminutive body to the deliverance of a brief but ferocious dad-hug.

I thought of my own grandkids thousands of miles away going through similar morning routines, making their own at-times-dramatic departures from their attentive and devoted parents.

There is, most assuredly, no hug like a tiny hug.

> *Millions and millions of years would still not give me half enough time to describe that tiny instant of all eternity when you put your arms around me and I put my arms around you.*
>
> —Jacques Prévert

A STUDY IN SANDSTONE

This morning found me sitting on the still-chilly banks of the Middle Fork River, contemplating. As is my routine, I had begun the Ritual of the Rocks: throwing four small rocks into the rippling, burbling waters. One for me and one for each of my three rock-throwing grandchildren.

As I held the fourth and final rock in my hand, I paused to feel its rough ridges and high points. I remember thinking, "In you go. Time to join a timeless interplay of liquid and solid. Your new environs will smooth out your rough edges."

After tossing this rock, I revisited my previous thought. "What about me? Am I a river rock or a terrestrial rock?" From there I considered the pros and cons of having my rough edges smoothed by decades' worth of experiences and encounters with other people.

Upon protracted reflection, I realized I do not want to be a river rock or a terrestrial rock. I have no desire to be a sociopath, disallowing and disavowing the influences of others—impervious, unyielding, inert. Neither do I want to lose my individuality, ending up submerged and worn down by interactions with my fellow “rocks,” ploddingly reduced to a conformed path of least resistance.

As is often the case, I decided the truth is somewhere in the middle—the middle fork, if you will.

The most beautiful rocks have faced the hardest waves.

—Kruti Joshi

TRIGGERS

Spending nine hours a day riding and working in a car with someone is a fast (though not always recommended) way to get to know a person. Such has been the case this week with my Canadian coworker here in Ontario. The first things I noticed about Lenny were his broad shoulders and easy, self-effacing manner.

Initially, we struggled to find common ground. What else would you expect from a couple of introverts? Lenny is the grandson of Lithuanian and Hungarian nickel miners, and the son of a sawmill worker. My new acquaintance attended college on a hockey scholarship; his scars and dental bridgework lend credence to his backstory.

For the first couple of days, our topics of conversation drifted haltingly from popular culture to a handful of mutual friends to the vacillating spring weather to our respective work-related adventures. Our first few meals together featured considerably more consumption than conversation.

Things abruptly changed at dinner tonight. After being seated by the hostess, we surveyed our menus, all the while keeping one eye on the big-screen television. Hockey. Playoff hockey. The Colorado vs. Dallas pre-game show was center stage for a restaurant full of Canadians. Then, suddenly and quite palpably, the expression on Lenny's face dropped. He disconnected from the menu, from me, from time and place. After a pronounced and awkward pause, I asked if he was okay. Summoned back to the present, Lenny pointed to the CBC's (Canadian Broadcasting Corporation) interrupting coverage of wildfires in the western provinces. We watched wordlessly—I with a sense of insulated curiosity and Lenny with a look of visceral familiarity.

During the course of the evening meal, Lenny uncomfortably related a memory ("the memory") from his teen years—specifically, the drought-induced Manitoba wildfires of 1989. "We lived in a small town near the mines. My family didn't have much, and when you don't have much to start with, it really hurts to lose it all." His childhood home had burned to the ground. Ditto for Nagymama's (Hungarian for grandmother) house two blocks away.

Lenny's family never recovered. They were seared emotionally and financially. For the remainder of his high school years, the family bounced from emergency shelters to disaster-recovery trailers to subsidized apartments. Throughout those turbulent years, Lenny shared a queen-sized bed with his younger brother and sister. "Sleep was the hardest part for years—forever waking in the middle of the night to peek out the window, sniff for smoke, then sit up to watch over my siblings. Hockey became my release, in part because being out on the middle of a frozen lake was as far away from fire as I could get—not just for me but for Stevie and Kaki as well. Kaki was really talented, but back then there weren't many opportunities for girls or women, so she ended up playing wing for the boys' high school team. Anyone who crossed her ended up getting a check from her, followed by a more vigorous check from Stevie."

Physically, Lenny remained at the table, but his gaze was far off. I knew my role. I bided my time and then sat and listened. I empathized. A bit later in Lenny's hotel room, we watched the first period of the game together. During breaks in the action, I shared a bit of my personal teen trauma and divulged a couple of my own memory triggers.

Our plan for tomorrow? I believe that I speak for Lenny when I say we will be ready to take on the world—together.

> *When people allow you to know about their pain and talk about it, take your shoes off. It's a holy place. Be humble, be kind when someone shows you vulnerability.*
>
> —Amani Albair

THE CHIEF CHILD CAR SEAT DESIGNER ADDRESSES THE NEW RECRUITS

Good morning, everyone.

Contrary to rumor, we do not design our car seats to be literally impossible to install. We tried that once, but the results were . . . how do I put this delicately? . . . a torrent of angry phone calls, irate parents at my doorstep, and one gentleman who threatened to "show me how he fits into tight spaces." It was not good for business.

Instead, we've spent decades perfecting something far more diabolical: a "challenge-based" approach. Our research shows that parents—particularly new ones—possess two things in abundance: spare time and a taste for punishment. Why else would anyone have children?

So our mission is to provide an activity that's less about safety and more about character-building. Imagine 3-D Tetris played with screaming toddlers as the soundtrack. That's our sweet spot.

For starters, the seats themselves must be unreasonably large—not just inconvenient but genuinely unwieldy. Ideally, they should behave like drunk refrigerators, shifting their weight at random intervals. And compatibility? We believe in mystery. Our newest model, the XL-500, fits seamlessly in the 2019, 2021, and 2024 Toyota Camrys, but not in 2020, 2022, or 2023. That's called free enterprise.

The beauty of our design is its ripple effect on the economy. Parents hire circus contortionists to wedge the seat into place, rodeo wranglers to cinch it down, and therapists to cope with the trauma. Entire industries flourish because of us.

And then, of course, there are the straps. Yes, they're adjustable, but not in any way that could be described as "reasonable." Ideally, tightening them should require a hydraulic winch or at least a pair of yoked Belgian draft horses.

As for the children, safety is important but curiosity is more so. That's why the harness release is designed to respond to the lightest possible touch—a finger, a nose, or even a stray French fry.

Within seconds, the little hellion will be roaming the dashboard, activating windshield wipers, and tugging at the hood release.

We're not just selling car seats. We're selling stories, trauma, and the occasional lawsuit.

Humor is mankind's greatest blessing.

—Mark Twain

TUESDAY, MID-MORNING

I had spent the previous evening weighed down by alarming political and constitutional developments. My state of mind, along with my spirit, was weighed down with perplexed consternation.

As good fortune would have it, the new day would be busy for Amy and me, riding herd on three spring-loaded grandchildren. The balm for my condition proved to be a prolonged scene, acted out for a small but appreciative audience. My seat for the impromptu performance was a rope swing under the spreading branches of an oak tree. The setting? A backyard filled to overflowing with my wife's family history dating back to 1954.

The leading actress? The appropriately named Grace, a four-year-old whirling dervish with a shock of blonde hair and a pair of rosy, freckled cheeks displaying a wide, mischievous grin as she ran barefoot through the still-dewy morning grass—the same grass so familiar to the toes of her mother, grandmother, and great-grandmother. The world was safe, filled with comforting calls of red-winged blackbirds and distant moos from the neighbors' cows. There were no burdens too heavy for this girl's small shoulders. She was, as usual, 100 percent in the moment.

She repeated her routine seven or eight times: climb up into my lap, urge me on with cries of "Faster, Poppy," leap to the ground, run the 50 yards to the small creek, observe and comment on the work of her two brothers, and then race back to report her findings to me. She ran with a sense of purpose between her great-grandmother's clothesline and the fence-row bluebird houses built by her great-grandfather.

For my part, I listened intently to her updates on dragonflies, frogs, crawdads, minnows, and (rather secondarily) her brothers. Aloud and to myself I uttered, "Little girl, I could watch you run all day long. All day"—a small miracle that felt like everything.

The day would end, as all days do, but the memory of my barefoot granddaughter in the grass, in a yard that felt like a hug, lingers on.

> *Remember to live while you are still alive. Remember to love while you still dare to.*
>
> —Garrison Keillor

SOME DAYS ARE DIAMONDS

Through the long days of spring and summer, Amy and I have found ourselves drawn again and again to the nearby community of Butchersville. It's not the kind of place that is ripe with modern conveniences, but it is blessed with a past that lingers. Just off Old Mill Road lies a (rare) flat expanse of land among hardwood-covered hills where a pasture has been repurposed into four verdant baseball fields.

On countless evenings we have lingered at the dusty margins of these fields, listening to the raspy voices of the old-timers—wistful folks who speak of coalfield baseball leagues with crystallized memories undiminished by the decades. Timeless tales of batter's box exploits performed by the exploited. Players and coaches who have long since faded into the mist.

For our eight-year-old grandson, these fields are a home away from home. His parents, along with his four biological grandparents, seemingly know (at the bare minimum) two generations of each and every family represented. His younger siblings (the four-year-old sister and the two-year-old brother) run ceaselessly between loved ones, newly found friends, and Sucrose Central (AKA the concession stand).

Ah, the concession stand. My old wildlife professor once explained that many predators hunt using an evolved technique known as "specific search image." For my grandchildren, the specific image is the Freezer Pop. The well-honed strategy? So glad that you asked. One grandchild distracts parents and grandparents while the other takes his or her cue and makes a break for Sucrose Central. Their timing, choreography, and posturing are brilliant—part ballet, part Capture the Flag.

At a mere twenty-five cents each, the brightly-colored, sugary treats fly out of the concession stand window with such regularity and frequency that the suckers—ahem—adults waiting in line at the stand are easy targets for wide-eyed, woefully neglected, wordlessly pleading preschoolers. Brazen behavior, but oh so effective. The two-year-old learned this not-so-proud tradition from the four-year-old who, in turn, learned it from the eight-year-old. Once the inevitable payoff has been secured, the pint-sized recipient scurries away to devour yet another freezer pop.

The story of Butchersville doesn't just live in swirls of memories. It continues in the exuberance of children, in the preponderance of sticky fingerprints, and in the manner a small community knows and cares for its offspring. In those fields, the years are seamless. On a summer evening, benevolence may find an uncredited part for you if you have lived a charmed life.

> *Since baseball time is measured only in outs, all you have to do is succeed utterly; keep hitting, keep the rally alive, and you have defeated time. You remain forever young.*
>
> —Roger Angell

SUMMER'S DAY WITH MY GIRL

I know, I know. I keep writing about my grandkids. No apologies here.

This afternoon, it was just me and the four-year-old, a tiny pocket of time carved out of the chaos of life. We sat on plastic chairs with the warm sun on our backs. With deliberate dedication, we worked our way through the ice cream cones that had been provided by the local shop. In response to my prodding, Grace told me about her day with the solemn sincerity only a four-year-old can muster.

And then, unsummoned, boom! Ever find yourself absorbed in a captivating movie when the soundtrack bleeds into the perfect song at the most opportune time? "Life is Sweet" by Natalie Merchant wafted from the shop's outdoor speakers.

"Why are you crying, Poppy?" my granddaughter asked, her rosy face full of ice cream and concern.

Sometimes love just spills over the edges. Sometimes joy, grief, and wonder all swirl together into . . . fullness. For a moment, everything felt exactly right and also unbearably fleeting.

So I just smiled, winked at her, and licked my ice cream.

Without ice cream, there would be darkness and chaos.
—Don Kardong

Questions? Comments? Suggestions?
Send a note to allen34cook@yahoo.com.

www.ingramcontent.com/pod-product-compliance
Lightning Source LLC
LaVergne TN
LVHW010607100826
845148LV00014B/2882